Drop Your Weapons:
The Kaz Chomko Story

Anna Elizabeth Carling

"If You Wish to be Brothers,

Drop Your Weapons."

Pope John Paul II

ISBN: 978-1-105-24501-5

Cover Design: Kayla Paloheimo
Editors: Gail Lennon and Anna-Marie Porcaro

Anna Elizabeth Carling
Email: ac9health@gmail.com
www.ahachi.com/transformation-and-enlightenment.html

Acknowledgments

Faith is like a language. It can have many different dialects. Some can seem altogether strange. But, if we are able find affinity with another person, we can communicate. The understanding of his or her particular faith then becomes easier. This is so because faith's knowledge rests in the sense of oneness, not the mind. I found that shared tone of faith with Kaz. I am thankful because it became the foundation for my listening to him and for the writing of this book.

In our discussions about the details of his life's story, most of my questions were based on the recorded notes of Elizabeth Chomko. These notes have been very helpful.

I appreciate being allowed to use the quotations of Pope John Paul II, Winston Churchill, Field-Marshall Montgomery, General Eisenhower, General Patton, and Saint Francis, as well as the Boy Scouts' pledge. The quotes have added to the flavour of each particular circumstance.

Some copies of the photos came from Kaz's personal shots. Some are from Hesperus' collection. For the bulk of the war-time pictures, I am indebted to Thadeusz

Wiatrowski, who published a collection of photos in 1946 called *Second Polish Armoured Regiment in Action – From Caen to Wilhelmshaven*. The credit for the picture of Pope John Paul II goes to Passiohaus-info.org.

Wikipedia, the free on-line encyclopedia, as well as the historical archives of the Canadian and Polish governments have been sources of war information.

Many people have shared their memories and expertise, and have given me encouragement. Most notable among them are: Susana Ochi, Marie Aretusi, Sybille Hahn, Heliane Hall, Ina Bruce, Eunice Podolski, Pina Corigliano and others, including the members of my family, especially Kayla Paloheimo, who designed the cover. Gail Lennon and Anna-Marie Porcaro assisted with editing. Allan Hughes is the reader of the audio version, recorded and edited by Chaim Gilad. The audio book includes Kaz's own voice answering my questions about the perils of WWII, and how he, by following his inner voice, emerged as an agent of peace.

My heartfelt thanks to you all, but most of all to the Guidance, which, when followed with commitment and trust, leads us toward Peace and Love's Glory. AC

Table of Contents

The Life in Ponure was not Sad

Two water buckets, carried from the creek after the day's work, were on a bench beside the door to the house. Each day, Adolf filled the basin beside one of them for himself and the boys for their wash. But, often, in the summer, Kazimierz the Great and Boleslaw the Bold (as their father sometimes teasingly called them after the ancient Polish kings) went to wash in the water hole by the fast-flowing stream which meandered through the farm property.

The surrounding forest with its hillocks and the meadows around the farms of Ponure made the environment seem peaceful. And, although the word *ponure* means sad, Kaz's childhood was not sad but happy and secure. In the early twentieth century, this part of the Podlaskie province had not been—apart from a lack of education for its inhabitants—affected by the frequent wars and border disputes which had been Poland's lot for hundreds of years.

The Chomko family was naturally devout. Mother Maria taught the boys and younger Sophia to know, inwardly, how to think and act. She taught them about God's constant presence and the penalty for doing wrong, but she also taught them about His love. The boys' father, Adolf, was good natured and hard-working, and grandfather Pavel taught Kaz to roam the forests without ever feeling lost.

Kazimierz was born in 1911. At that time, Poland was a part of the Czar's empire. Because it was heavily influenced by the Russians, regular schooling started only after Poland's independence in 1920. "Russians did not believe in educating peasants, and only a few people knew how to read or write," said Kaz.

In this rural province, the ancestors were part of its very soil—not so much in terms of the location, but in the way their life was lived. Kaz did not know when and from where the ancestors of the Chomko clan had come to Ponure. If any church records had been kept, they had been lost. However, he recalled hearing about a soldier named Chomko who had served in the entourage of a Lithuanian Princess. This was, supposedly, long before his great grandfather had settled in Ponure. Here, each generation had brought something innovative to the simple life.

Pioneering of the farm land was done by Kaz's great grandfather who had been a forester, taking care of the surrounding government lands. The local inhabitants were poor. They poached forbidden animals for food and cut down even big trees for firewood. The forest ranger roamed the forests to keep this from happening. He also ensured that the rich undergrowth was cleared so that more valuable trees such as: oak, pine, linden and elm would have a better chance to grow. After twenty five years in the service of the Russian Czar Alexander II, Kaz's great grandfather had been granted forty acres of prime forest, a part of which he cleared in order to create a homestead for his family.

Clearing the ground, at that time, was a slow process. In addition to cutting down the trees, wrestling the roots out of the ground, and burning them before the open land became a fertile field, the soil had to be tilled to make it productive. This meant ploughing, harrowing, planting seeds, and tending the crop. Building the farm house and the barn involved sawing and shaping the wood into logs. This was all done using only a handsaw, a chisel, and a knife. The logs had to be allowed to age before they were used as building material.

Most likely, the forester had some help from the neighbours. He must have had a horse for pulling the roots from the ground and for transporting the logs for the buildings. Little by little, the homestead took shape. Calves were raised to become milk-producing cows. Chickens were bought or bartered to produce eggs. A cellar was dug to preserve root vegetables such as: potatoes, beets, carrots, and turnips.

Grandfather Pavel diverted the stream which ran through the property. He dug a hole big enough for a plank to be placed on it for washing laundry. The clothes were first soaked, then placed on top of the plank one by one, and then scrubbed with a large brush and homemade soap. They were rinsed first in the waterhole which was a few feet deep and had a solid clay bottom so that the water stayed relatively clear. The final rinse was done in the flowing stream. The clothes were spread on the ground or nearby bushes for drying in the sun. On rainy days, they were carried to the attic to be hung on the clotheslines. And, well, in the winter time, doing the laundry was not that easy!

Each succeeding generation added its contribution. Pavel, in addition to providing facilities for washing the laundry, built a few bee hives behind the farm house to supply the family with honey. Kaz's father rebuilt and expanded the barn as well as the root cellar. The dugout sauna, built into a hillock not far from the stream, was the contribution of Vincenty, Adolf's younger brother, after he returned from the war, in 1920. Vincenty spent two years at his childhood home before getting married and setting up a household of his own on the other half of the farm property.

During the war years, the areas where the army units were stationed for long periods of time were often in the middle of a forest. Hiding from the enemy was easier there than in open spaces. The soldiers were ingenious about finding ways to live as normal lives as possible. One of them, of course, was keeping themselves clean. Thus, the dugout saunas became a part of the day-to-day war ritual. Water had to be near and accessible. Usually, it was a stream similar to the one running through the Chomko lands.

For the sauna, small trees around the chosen place had to be cut down and shaped to become the support beams for the small cave, which had already been dug. The side and overhead beams were secured to prevent cave-ins. Rough benches were set up against the back wall. The grate for holding the burning logs was constructed from metal, usually from a piece of army equipment that had been partially destroyed. After the grate was set up, rocks about the size of a man's fist were placed around and on it. With no chimney, the slanting door was kept partly open so the smoke could escape during the wood burning phase. The rocks had to be hot enough to sizzle when water was thrown on them. They, then, would retain the heat for several hours. When the stones were hot enough, the door was closed. The sweat lodge was ready for its first bathers. The water had to be brought in buckets, which, in some places, were rigged up with ropes to create a rudimentary shower for scrubbing off dirt with soapy water. If a pond or stream was close, swimming was the first choice for the rinse. In the winter, bathers resorted to rolling in the snow.

After the war, the gatherings by the dug-out sauna on the farm became customary for the Chomkos. Vincenty told war stories, which made young boys' imaginations soar. This was especially true of Bobe, who began to dream of a military career.

But, Bobe understood little of the atrocities of war. He did not know that, in this war alone, which had resulted from Russian attempts to carry the revolution westward, over 200,000 Polish troops had fought against the armies of Russia. He was unaware that tens of thousands had been killed and even larger numbers of Polish civilians had been moved to labour camps.

Combining the numbers of the Russian and Austrian-Hungarian war, the military and civilian deaths were

estimated to be over a million. The plundering retreat strategies had left much of the war zone uninhabitable. Finally, after four years of fighting and devastation of the countryside, local governments had been created one by one. Only when they pledged allegiance to the central government in Warsaw, was the reality of the independence affirmed. Poland had been under the yoke of foreign tyranny for 123 years. The new border which corresponded roughly to the 1793 frontier, cut across mixed Ukrainian and Belarusian territories.

"Previous to the liberation," Kaz recalled, "we were safe in our home. The family listened daily to the crystal radio to keep informed about the progress of the Polish army. I have some vague recollections of the war against the Bolsheviks. They were marching hard on Warsaw. I think they were after Polish wine and cigarettes more than anything else! But, really, they weren't an army. They were more like a bunch of hoodlums. Thankfully, they never achieved their goal. There was even a story circulating that, when the

Russians were trying to cross the Wistula River, a miracle in the form of Virgin Mary appeared, and thousands of them drowned."

In August 1920, a battle raged in and around Warsaw between Polish and Bolshevik forces. At stake was the future of Poland. Red Army commanders made a tactical error when a large part of their force diverted north of Warsaw in order to cut Polish supply lines from the Baltic Sea. The Poles set a trap, taking full advantage of the Russians' error. Consequently, the diverted Red Army became cut off from its own supply line and the remaining force was nearly destroyed. Many regarded this turn of events as a miracle. It became known as the Miracle on Wistula. The Red Army was so badly defeated that it began to retreat on all fronts. The Polish forces chased the Bolshevik forces using all manner of weaponry, including armour. This showed that tanks could play a role in rapid advances on the battlefield.

Finally, Poland was free. The armistice was signed on October 12, 1920.

Vincenty's stories excited the young boys. But, it was their gentle and quiet mother who demonstrated in her life the power of faith and the hope that comes from that faith. She often reminded the family members that problems cannot be solved without the inner guidance. By following its promptings, God's power becomes visible through our thoughts and actions. This way, Maria shaped the family's religious beliefs and gave a spiritual tone to the Chomko family.

On Saturday evenings, Maria made sure that everyone had clean clothes ready for the Sunday mass, which the family attended without fail. The church was in Wasilkuw, a town that had emerged around a stopping place for state coaches travelling to Moscow. The seven kilometres to church was covered by walking or by riding on the wagon platform with the low side panels, drawn by Massi, the horse. The adults had the front seat and the children sat at the back on the hard platform. This made their backsides sore since the dirt road was bumpy. Later, when Kaz received his first bike, riding this path to the church was a breeze.

 The Bishop's visit to the church was very special. Mother talked about it for weeks ahead of time. Once, when Kaz was about ten years of age, he had a strange experience during the mass. Sitting in a pew beside his father and listening to the choir, Kaz

fixed his eyes on the stained glass window which reflected the sunlight into many colours.

It was so beautiful that he could not take his eyes off the light. Suddenly, he felt as if he was that light, shining above everyone in the congregation.

When the service was over, he followed the others out to the church yard. He still felt light and peaceful. Everything around him seemed extra bright. The green leaves of trees shimmered, and the colours of flowers in the bushes were more alive than ever before. He felt as if he was a walking translucent, like some holy thing. Although he never spoke to anyone about this experience, it remained in his memory for a long time. Recalling it gave him comfort and served him well whenever he felt scared or sad. It even helped to make him less sad when he remembered his grandfather who had died two years earlier.

 The workday finished at dusk. That's when father led the horse into the barn, and forked hay for it and

the cows which had already had their second milking of the day. Mother poured most of the milk into a container with a lid, then tied a long rope on the handle of the container and lowered it into the well to keep it cool. The rest of the milk was consumed with the supper. Sour milk was processed overnight. It was then eaten in the morning along with gruel or a type of muesli. The milk which had become jelly-like with a creamy covering, when eaten with sugar and sometimes cinnamon on top, tasted delicious.

Kaz and Bobe helped pasture the cows on the farm land reserved for grazing. Some of the grazing land was also owned by the government. The latter land had areas planted with young saplings. The young herders had to be mindful of the cattle throughout the day in order to keep the cows from eating or trampling the young trees which would not survive such an onslaught.

In order to store hay for the winter, Adolf used a scythe, and sometimes a sickle in less accessible places. Nothing was left on the fields to rot. The cut hay was spread on the ground for a few days to dry. Then, it was raked into piles for transporting.

One day, the whole family was in the distant hayfield where the hay had been raked and piled high into the wagon. Massi pulled it to the home barn. The boys were doing their favourite work in the hayloft. They were jumping on the newly-mowed hay that was to be stored for the winter. Compressing the hay into as small a space as possible was more play than work for them.

"Look, Kaz!" cried Bobe, as he hung from the rafters, then swung himself down on top of the hay. Although two years younger than ten-year-old Kaz, Boleslaw was the more adventurous of the two brothers. He had climbed the rungs of the ladder at the far end of the barn and hoisted himself onto a rafter, like a monkey.

A latched opening at the end of the hayloft was used to shovel the amount of hay needed for the cows and the horse housed underneath. The pig had its own pen and the chickens were in another section where they could go outside through a small opening to a fenced area. There, the rooster crowed each morning, waking everyone at dawn.

As the sun was setting, after a rigorous work day, supper was served in the large kitchen/living area. The plates were arranged in their designated places on a long, wooden table. Ravenously hungry, the boys ate potatoes and ham, which had been marinated and then cured in the smokehouse. Pieces of cured ham were stored in the attic along with other necessities such as garlic and herbs. In the summer fresh greens were also part of the meal.

The root cellar, located close to the house, had a slanting latch door. A smaller door inside led to a shelved area big enough to store potatoes, carrots, beets and other root vegetables as well as preserves for the winter months.

For many reasons, the attic was Kaz's favourite place. It was great for hiding from Bobe. It was also a good place for him to do his thinking about life and what he was learning. He often thought of his Grandfather Pavel who was no longer there to guide Kaz with his wise council. When his grandfather was still alive, he seemed to have had a relevant answer for everything that was puzzling to a young boy.

At times, Kaz missed him terribly. But, he could not talk about his feelings of desperation with anyone. While in the attic, he would recall some of their explorations through the beautiful forest. He and his grandfather had climbed rocky hills together. Once, they had seen an eagle's nest where the mother bird had just returned to feed her young. There, up high, they had sat in silence until Pavel said to Kaz, "By being silent with nature, we hear nature giving us knowledge of heaven." When he asked Pavel about this knowledge, Pavel said, "Yes, it is a great wonder, and we must always question. Then, the answers come through intuition and faith."

After a pause his grandfather continued, "Never let your faith falter because of what human beings do! The power of faith helps you see God's wisdom within every question and every problem. This leads to the right solution. What is more, step by step it will bring you to a growing understanding of this paradox of life!"

Unfortunately, Kaz did not often get an opportunity to go to the attic to think or daydream. Jobs around the house were plentiful and strictly assigned. He had to carry wood for the stove and haul water from the well. The toughest job was helping his father cut down a large tree. Kaz had learned to use the axe before he was ten. Now, it was his task to chop a wedge on the side of the tree. Afterwards, a double-handled saw was used. Kaz sawed on one side of the tree and Adolf on the other. At the exact moment before the tree fell, his father pointed in the direction to which Kaz was to run while his father circled the tree quickly in order to avoid being hurt. Some trees were really high. But, accidents were avoided. The fallen tree was next stripped of its branches. These were chopped for firewood along with the trunk, provided it was not needed as building material. Smaller pieces of wood were sometimes used as material for carving spoons and bowls. In the evenings, a splinter of wood was dipped in lard and lit to give some light. Kerosene was too expensive to use every day. It was used only when it was really needed for some specific work.

One of the earliest memories Kaz recalled was sitting on his grandfather's lap in the rocking chair in the semi-dark living room. Pavel had carved and given him a small wooden horse. Mother was removing breads from the oven with a flat scoop. The yeasty smell of fresh-baked bread filled the room. Kaz listened to the grandfather's rhythmic humming. This memory always symbolized happiness from Kaz's early childhood.

Kaz followed his grandfather wherever he could, even when he was older. One day, they went, together, to collect honey from the beehives which Pavel kept behind the fence. Kaz was not allowed to cross the fence lest he be stung. Grandfather wore a veil hanging from a wide hat when he collected the honey.

Traveling Jewish merchants from Bialystock (an industrial centre that focused on textiles such as blankets and overcoats) came along with their wagons. They waited by the fence for grandfather to finish collecting the honey. Suddenly, one of them cried, "Oh! A bee stung me!"

Grandfather said, "Kaz, run to the kitchen and ask your mother for a piece of cloth and a mug of cold water." When Kaz returned, the man was asked to drink some water. The cloth was dipped in the rest of it, and then placed on the wrist where the bee sting was now red. As the pain subsided, grandfather remarked, "Perhaps you should not eat so many onions! Bees don't like onions."

Flu hit the family one winter day. Kaz felt a cold coming on. He was sneezing, and he felt tired and foggy. Someone had told him that garlic was a good remedy. He climbed to the attic, where the garlic strings hung, peeled a whole compound bulb and ate every single part. His stomach hurt and he had to drink lots of water to overcome the pain. But, he was cured. Kaz has used garlic as an all-round remedy ever since.

Learning to work when he was young gave Kaz strength. By the time he was ten, his father gave him a small allowance, which the boy saved from one week to the next to buy a bicycle. He finally got the bike when he was eleven. From then on, it was much easier to get to church on Sunday, to deliver cream to the village shop and, of course, it was much easier to get to school.

During the First World War, the schools were closed. Learning to read and write at home was not an option since neither parent knew how read or write. The boys saw books only when they visited their cousins. As soon as the war was over, the boys' mother took them to the school in Charnaviecz (a town along the main railway line between Warsaw and Moscow). In the beginning, this meant a two-hour walk each way. Kaz didn't mind it for he was eager to learn. Peaceful by nature, he did what he was told—and that was to keep his attention to learning.

For Bobe, going to school was not as interesting as playing pranks. Climbing trees was his favourite pastime. Whenever he was supposed to help his older brother and wasn't doing so, Kaz knew exactly where to find him. He would often be found sitting on the lower branch of a pine tree with a slingshot in his hand. He knew better than to shoot at anything moving on the ground. He was quite accurate at hitting stationary targets. Bobe wanted to go into the military, to become a commanding officer. But, later, he changed his mind and planned to go into the medical corps.

Schooling and Helping Aunt Stephania

When Kaz was nearly thirteen, his Aunt Stephania approached his parents about having Kaz as her helper. She owned a restaurant but was not able to manage it on her own. She had married a man whose shady dealings forced him to leave the country. He had gone to America, Kaz overheard, never to be seen again. Aunt Stephania said that now that Kaz could read and write, he could keep her books after school. That would be a great help. Bobe could take up Kaz's chores and become more responsible in helping around the farm. After long negotiations, the boys' parents agreed.

What were Kaz's feelings about the subject? Until then, he had always been agreeable, particularly to his parent's wishes. He had been very close to his grandfather, who always gave wise advice. But his grandfather was no longer there to give advice and none of his many sayings that had stayed in Kaz's memory were of help. Proverbs such as: *Feed your dogs before you take them for hunting* or *You can lead a horse to water but you cannot make him drink* were of no help to him in his present predicament.

Unaccustomed to opposing anyone except Bobe with whom he had quarrels every now and then, Kaz did not express his opinion. However, he felt some excitement about his immediate future. He moved to Czarnawiecs, into the attic room in his aunt's house. Aunt Stephania could read but not write. Therefore, Kaz wrote down all the day's transactions. Once a week, he added up what each customer owed to her. The bills were generally paid on time for Aunt Stephania never forgot anything.

Kaz was kept busy after the school. He swept the floors and helped his aunt with cooking and washing dishes. School was going well. He had made new friends who invited him to join the Boy Scouts. He did so against his aunt's wishes. At scout meetings and outings, he learned many survival techniques like: how to survive in the wilderness and how to light a fire with a flint. Kaz enjoyed mixing with the boys who shared his views on life. He hung the copy of the Scout Oath on the wall of his room:

> *On my honour I will do my best*
> *To do my duty to God and my country*
> *and to obey the Scout Law;*
> *To help other people at all times;*
> *To keep myself physically strong,*
> *mentally awake, and morally straight.*

Account keeping and other special jobs Kaz did at the restaurant did not take much of his time. Kaz began to help at the back where Stephania's friend, Andre, had set up a butcher shop. The pigs, goats, and sheep were brought in already skinned. The butcher cut them into sections, storing the lard separately. The sections and the lard were picked up by his customers, who either used the meat immediately or marinated and smoked it later in their own smoke houses. Alternately, the meat was salted in barrels for winter use. Kaz was fascinated by the entire process. He enjoyed learning the butcher's job. Whenever he could, he was at the back of the restaurant. There, he could eat as much kielbasa as he wanted. He also earned good pocket money, which he saved to buy gifts for his visits home.

Kaz became aware that Aunt Stephania had more than a business relationship with Andre. Whenever the butcher was inebriated, having drunk too much beer, Andre became jealous. A few German soldiers frequented the restaurant. One of them had taken a fancy to Stephania. The two of them had secret meetings in the hayloft. Nothing was mentioned about this until, one evening, the butcher, having had too many bottles of beer that had been heated on the stove, began to argue with Stephania. Their altercation would have resulted in physical injuries without Kaz's interference. Luckily, by that time, he was already a strong and mature teenager. He never mentioned the incident to anyone for, as he put it, "I did not want to gossip!"

The Chomko family had many interactions. Some of the family members were close to each other. Kaz often wondered how his mother must have felt when his father had told her that his first choice for marriage had been mother's sister, Stephania. Mother had always been quiet and gracious about it, the same way as she was about all her other challenges. Kaz's father always treated his wife respectfully. He valued her wisdom, patience, and unswerving faith. In her quiet way, she was the one who determined how the family lived.

Kaz was eager to learn about life, including school work. The more he learned, the more sense of freedom he felt as he moved about the village on his bike. Poland had only recently gained its independence and since the eastern part had been under the Russian domination, the older people had not had opportunities to learn reading or writing. They learned about world events from other villagers, from passing travelers, or by listening to the rudimentary crystal radio. Since Kaz's parents did not know how to read or write, his ability was valuable not only for adding the accounts, but also for reading the news and keeping in touch with other family members.

Working in the restaurant came to an end when Kaz's sixth grade schooling was finished. The school did not have higher grades and Kaz was needed at the farm. Conflict between his father and Stephania developed. Father needed help on the farm and Stephania claimed that she could not manage the restaurant without Kaz. She even indicated that the restaurant would be his when she retired. "Who knows?" she said shrugging. "Perhaps, one day, I'll leave and go to America and you'll inherit what I have," she told Kaz.

It was suggested that one of Kaz's siblings could help her at the restaurant. Sophia was four years younger and a good helper around the house. Finally, it was agreed that she would now move to Aunt Stephania's house. This worked out well. Sophia became the helper. Later, she inherited Aunt Stephania's house with the restaurant.

Father needed and wanted Kaz back at the farm. But Kaz felt that since further schooling was not possible he would look for work somewhere nearby where he could enjoy his independence. Kaz wanted to work in the forest and still be able to help on the farm. He approached the forest ranger working in the area and became his helper in clearing the undergrowth and keeping watch on poachers.

The farmers in the eastern provinces had always been poor. Now they were paying taxes to the Polish government. But, earlier the land had been owned by the nobles. Each year, the farmer had been compelled to pay rent for using the land. Throughout history, most of the peasants had continued as 'earth serfs'.

In 1861, during the reign of Czar Alexander II, the serfdom had been finally abolished. He listened to a petition presented by the Polish proprietors who wanted their relations with the serfs regulated in a more satisfactory way. The Czar authorized the formation of committees for the improving the condition of the peasants in all of Russia and laid down the principles for practical improvements. Alexander had to choose between the different recommendations. Should the serfs become agricultural labourers, dependent economically and administratively on the landlords? Or, should they be transformed into a class of independent proprietors? The emperor gave his support to the latter proposal and the Russian peasantry became one of the last groups of peasants in Europe to shake off serfdom.

About the same time, Kaz's great grandfather was working for the government as a forester and was granted, after twenty-five years of service, the forty acres of land where the Chomko farm now existed.

Seasoning through Army Discipline

Papers ordering Kaz to report to the army headquarters in the nearby town arrived. Kaz was washing himself after the day's work in the forest when Bobe ran toward him. He shook the envelope excitedly while Kaz dried his face on a towel hanging on a clothesline. They sat on a rock while Kaz read the orders. He was to go to the town recruitment centre where he would receive the papers needed for the physical exam. If he passed the exam, he would, then, be directed to his army unit.

Healthy, even robust, Kaz had no reservations when he was sitting waiting for his exam. As he walked in the doctor looked at him intently and said, "Looks like you will be a good addition to the Polish army. Are you ready for a change in your life? What is your occupation now?"

"I have been helping a forest ranger close to my father's farm where I also work on week-ends." Kaz answered.

Listening with his stethoscope to Kaz's chest he remarked, "No problem here!"

Kaz returned to the front desk where he received papers to fill in details about his life experiences. He was also given a choice of preferred units: infantry, artillery, or navy. The length for infantry training was a year and a half, artillery two years, and for the navy, it was three. Not knowing too much about any of them Kaz chose the artillery.

Eager to learn, the way he had always been when presented challenges, he put his heart into this new challenge in his life. In his free time, he visited the headquarters' library where he sat for hours in the reading room learning theory. He learned that the field artillery is a category of mobile units used to support the armies in the field. The weapons are specialized for mobility, proficiency, long range, short range, and extremely long range target engagement.

Previously, field artillery was also known as foot artillery. The guns were pulled by horses and the gun crews marched on foot, thus providing fire support to the infantry. Now motor vehicles towed the guns, carried the crews, and transported the ammunition. He learned about other heavy artillery, what constituted the grades and their range distance.

Kaz learned about shot guns, revolvers, hunting guns, and in what circumstances they could be used. At the practice range, he was taught how to hold a rifle and how to aim it in order to hit the target. The cardboard target was in a human form. This gave Kaz pause. But he had no time to think as he was pressed to follow the orders of the shouting sergeant to aim and hit the target.

Only when he was lying awake on his bed at night was it possible for him to think about the question of 'right to kill'. Could he, with clear conscience, hit the target if it was a living, breathing, human being? Kaz felt a shudder go through him with the thought. He could not think clearly yet he felt uncomfortable even considering the topic of taking the life of another.

The priest had talked about this with the young boys and questions such as: *Should Christians involve themselves in warfare?* had arisen. What about defending our homeland, our fragile independence as a nation, our culture, and our beliefs? Russians under the Communist rule did not share these beliefs. What would happen if they were impossible to practice? So many unanswered questions emerged in Kaz's mind, many of them difficult to put into words at that time yet he felt them stirring within.

Living conditions in the old army barrack were intolerable. Kaz's bed with his belongings underneath was one of two dozen rickety beds in a long room on the fourth floor of an old barrack. It was sometimes a real challenge to run fast enough to get to the outdoor toilet on time.

At night, if one of the 'inmates' had not folded his uniform and polished his boots 'just so', every one of the new recruits had to get up, stand in line while being yelled at by a sergeant. Then, they had to refold their uniforms, polish their boots, and, again, be inspected. Often, in the middle of the night, when everyone was sleep, the sergeant would march in and yell, "Attention!" Everyone was expected to respond from a deep sleep in seconds.

This went on for weeks. Since every day was also filled with ruthless discipline, the young soldiers experienced exhaustion, anger and rage, then hopelessness. Many would have preferred to die. But there was no time to commit suicide. All this discipline was training to build character, Kaz was told.

After three months of the cruel treatment some of the soldiers, including Kaz, were transferred to a non-commissioned army school. There, life became a bit easier. However, rigorous war exercises were extensive in this school which trained corporals and sergeants of various ranks. These are officers with authority given by a commissioned officer. Therefore, they do not carry the same responsibilities as higher ranking officers. However, non-commissioned officers play an important role in the military operations because they train recruits and act as a liaison between commissioned officers and regular soldiers. They inform their superiors about situations of relevance and assist in many administrative tasks.

The discipline in the school was inherited from the former Austro-Hungarian empire which had ruled most of Europe for centuries. To have a well-trained army was important since Poland's new independence was fragile against the rising power of Communist rule in the Soviet Union and budding Nazi ambitions in Germany. Throughout history, Poland had had to be on guard. Czarist Russia had held a tight grip on its vassals. It was only when the turbulent revolution took place and the Czarist government was overthrown in 1918, that the smaller countries around it asserted themselves and gained independence as the result of the tumult. In the non-commissioned army school no one ever questioned the importance of tough discipline.

But now, the trainees were given more free time. This gave them opportunities to practice hobbies such as playing soccer or table tennis. Closer sharing of feelings or getting to really know the fellow compatriots did not happen. Feelings were kept private and the soldiers had little opportunity to develop a sense of camaraderie. Most of the men learned to hide their feelings covering them in jokes and forced laughter. Only in the darkness of the night, when there was no one to talk to, did these forbidden feelings emerge. That then resulted in sleepless nights. Homesick and fearful soldiers gazed at crumbled or faded photographs and longed for loved ones. Denying these emotions was impossible but sharing them would have seemed a weakness. This kind of pondering was even worse during the free hours when time seemed to drag with nothing to do.

Kaz had time to write letters to his parents, who received them via Sophia now living at Aunt Stephania's house and attending school as well as helping at the restaurant. But Kaz had never learned to share his feelings with his family members either. In his childhood home what he felt about people was never discussed. Mother worked hard looking after and feeding the family. Any free time she had after the hard labour of cleaning, gardening, milking the cows, carrying water and attending the cooking fire, she spent knitting or darning socks or making preserves. Using the millstone to grind the grain was also her job. All she did was work. There was no time or need for talking. Caring for the family and keeping them fed was deemed more than sufficient to show his parents' feelings.

No one ever asked each other, "How are you or what's troubling you?" If you were angry or sad, you were simply left to brood or perhaps given an extra treat such as candy from a jar in the cupboard.

When Kaz was sent to Aunt Stephania it was not his choice. He did what he was told. And that became a way of life in school, in the restaurant after school and, later, in the military. Kaz was used to taking orders and being quiet about his inner life and his feelings.

A new Direction and Romance

Discharge papers in their hands, Kaz and Alex, who had become friends during the two-year army training, sat in the cafeteria wondering what was in store for them. Alex spoke about going to Warsaw and finding a job in the newspaper business. He wanted to become a journalist. Kaz, whose education had started late and was limited to six years, had as his options: to go back to Stephania's restaurant or return to the farm where his father always needed an extra hand. At this point, he did not know which to choose. True to his character, he took a wait-and-see attitude.

Finally, he decided to visit Aunt Stephania. She was overjoyed to see him, and treated him like her own son. She offered the restaurant, and house to him, if he stayed. He declined. Inwardly, he knew that his life's role was not to stay and run a steady business. He suggested that she make the same offer to his sister, Sophia.

Kaz returned home to help his father while thinking of his next move. He had enjoyed helping the forest ranger. He loved that part of Poland with its beautiful forests and abundant game. Poaching was still a problem since the locals hunted forbidden game and cut down trees without permission. Also, Kaz liked the idea of spending time alone while roaming the land. Even as a child, he had enjoyed taking the cows to the government-own fields where he had to keep a close eye on them to prevent them from trampling on saplings that had been planted.

He applied for the job of a forester and was accepted. Again, his work area was close enough to the farm so that he could live at home and help his father in his spare time. This was important, particularly during the harvest season, since his younger brother, Bobe, had volunteered to go to the army when he was seventeen. (Bobe had become a paramedic. But, he was soon captured by the Nazis and sent to work on a farm in Germany. He spent most of the Second World War as a prisoner. Later, he settled back on the family farm with his enterprising Ukrainian wife, whom he had met while in Germany. They had four children and a few years after the war the Communist government allowed them to exchange the farm for an apartment in the nearby town.)

Learning about trees and helping them flourish was enjoyable to Kaz. But, at times, it was challenging when heavy undergrowth had to be cut down or when the remains of the tree had to be cleared, piled, and removed to the areas accessible for further transportation. Learning as he worked, Kaz became an expert in knowing where new saplings were to be planted in order to give them more growing space. He loved the clear mornings when he saw majestic pines casting their long shadows on the land, and squirrels playing hide and seek with him as he walked.

On Saturdays, he helped his father with the farm. After supper, he sometimes bicycled to the village to meet friends. It was on one of these outings that he met Maria, a sister of Valec Mackowsky, with whom he worked. Valec had spoken about his favourite sister often as they walked through the woods. But, since Kaz seldom joined in these Saturday outings, it was almost a year before the meeting took place.

On arrival, Kaz saw groups of young people around a refreshment stand close to an empty dance platform which stood amongst the birch trees. The sky was clear and the stars were beginning to twinkle. A fiddler was tuning his instrument. More young people gathered around the platform which had been erected years earlier for these summer dance events.

Placing his bicycle against a tree, Kaz wandered toward his friend on the other side of the platform, where Valec was talking to someone else. Close to him stood a young girl with dark, braided hair hanging over her shoulder.

Kaz stopped in wonder. He had never seen such a beautiful girl! Time stopped. He did not know how long he stood there, but, as their eyes met, he smiled. He felt that she was not a stranger. He finally went to his friend, who introduced her as his sister Maria.

Not much of a dancer, Kaz did not ask her to dance with him. Instead, he invited her to walk amongst the trees. When Kaz offered his hand to her, she smiled and shyly lifted her eyes to meet his. Sitting on a bench near a refreshment stand, they sipped their lemonade while surveying the scene. Not knowing what to say or ask, Kaz finally turned to her and said, "Your brother told me that you like sewing?"

Suddenly animated, Maria said enthusiastically, "Yes, our dad bought us a machine and I am learning to use it. Have you seen how it's used?"

"Yes, our house is so different now that my mother has made curtains by using the sewing machine. She makes father's shirts with the machine, too," Kaz told her.

"For me, it has been difficult to learn to make good patterns," she confessed. "But, I have a friend who is very good at it. She made the pattern for this dress."

Kaz looked at her and said, "It's really beautiful. It matches your blue eyes. You are beautiful," he added. Looking embarrassed, she smiled. They sat silent for a long time, sipping their drinks.

During the following week, Kaz saw Maria's beautiful face in his mind's eye. He relived their meeting, and he looked forward to the following Saturday when they were to meet in the same place. On the evening, when they walked hand in hand through the moon-lit forest and when Kaz had courage to kiss her, she did not resist. Maria remarked, "I feel as if we have always been together." For her, they did not even have to touch each other for that feeling to remain. Week by week their feelings for each other grew.

When Maria came to visit Kaz's home, his mother, also called Maria, did not say anything. But Kaz could see how much she liked the girl who had helped prepare the evening meal. When she became more familiar with the members of Kaz's family, young Maria came to visit often. On moonlit nights, the couple wandered along the stream or rested in haystacks while looking at the stars. On one of these nights, they began to dream about their future.

Kaz had been working as a forest ranger for two years and he did not see his future in that work. Younger men with special education in forestry were applying for jobs. Kaz felt that, soon, he would be squeezed out. He was, therefore, looking around for other opportunities.

One day when he was visiting Valec, he happened to meet a school friend on the street. The friend was well dressed and confident. Kaz asked, "What made the lady of fortune smile on you?"

The friend told him how he had joined the police force two years earlier, had undergone training, and now had a well-paying job in the city. Well, this appealed to Kaz. He applied to the same school and, although he was short of admission requirements, he was accepted, provided he upgraded his education during the training.

Maria was anxious to get married. Kaz liked her but was not so eager to get married. However, true to his amiable nature, he agreed to become engaged. They were to marry after police school was finished. In the meanwhile, she was to learn professional sewing with the seamstress in the village. Young Maria's hopes were high for sharing the joys and sorrows of a lifetime with her beloved.

During his second year of training in August of 1938, Kaz was visiting his fiancée. They spent an evening with Valec and his girlfriend who knew about a Gypsy fortune teller living on the outskirts of the town. Out of curiosity, each one had a private session with the seer. Not taking it seriously at the time, Kaz learned that he would not be in Poland for long, but would travel to a far-away country, perhaps overseas. Laughing about such an absurd prediction, the group left to continue their merry-making.

A few days later, a telegram arrived. Kaz was ordered immediately to return to his school. It was a simple order with no explanation, although, for months, rumours had been circulating about the threat of a possible German invasion of Poland. At the short farewell meeting with his girlfriend neither one could imagine that it was the last time they would see each other. Leaving his childhood home was the same. There were no tears or any sense that this was to be the final farewell to his parents. With a simple goodbye, Kaz threw his bag over his shoulder and left.

The Sounds of Impending War Drums

Fear of losing Poland's young independence had now become widespread. In the east, the Soviet Union had gained power as a Communist state. In the west, Hitler's armies were ready to strike to expand his power. Rumours about kidnappings, torture, and hangings were circulating everywhere in Poland. Yet, on the surface everything, was peaceful—at least in the area where Kaz was stationed for his practical training.

Two distinct nationalities existed in this southern border town of Rosdolo. For years, hostilities had led to fights, even murders between the Ukrainians and the Polish, who felt that Ukrainians were still, after several generations, Russian invaders. Police officers had confiscated several guns from the revolutionary types, who expected help from both sides and supposedly were planning murders and kidnappings. Police had to be on constant guard. A re-enforcement unit arrived one day to arrest the suspected instigators of the troubles.

For Kaz, patrolling the territory on bike in Rosdolo was enjoyable, in the beginning. He left early in the morning to cover the outskirts of the town, where he watched children chattering as they walked to their schools. Women in long skirts carried baskets on their way from the market, their shawls wrapped tightly around their shoulders to ward off the chill. As colourful leaves fluttered down in the fall breeze, Kaz enjoyed bicycling leisurely through the parks lanes during his shift of duty. "Rosdolo (Rosedale) was a pretty town," he remembered.

But because the town was close to the Russian border, the police presence was strong and the need for action could change rapidly. Also, jealousies developed between the older police officers and the young trainees since the veterans felt that they carried all the responsibilities, while the young ones enjoyed the town and gained popularity with its residents, particularly among the Polish sector.

Kaz recalled, "In the early years the Austrian-trained police dominated. They were corrupt – easily bribed and bought off. When the police force was reformed in 1936, it was informed by the government that the army would control it in the event of war. This meant that we continued with weapons training in order to be prepared. I remember hearing a lot of rumours during the build up to the war. But, no one really knew when it was going to happen or how. In fact, it came as a terrible shock when the invasion started. The country wasn't prepared. We had a defense treaty with Britain and France. They would attack Germany if Poland was invaded. I think we were relying on this as a deterrent."

Rumours were spread about German and Russian spies infiltrating the population. Speculations about Germany's plan to invade Poland increased month by month. Fear spread through whispers about manhunts by the Germans which had already taken place in the larger cities such as Warsaw. However, while it was a daily topic, many still took it as a political propaganda.

But, the Nazis did invade Poland on September 1, 1939. (See the arrival of the German troops). Kaz learned from the people who were fleeing that executions and other atrocities took place when the invaders encountered opposition from the Home Army which operated to protect Poland's freedom.

In Rosdolo, the young police officers were ordered to abandon their posts, given six month's salary in advance, and were told to report to the provincial headquarters in Stanislaw. The answer to the speculations as to why the urgent move came one step at a time. The young men were to travel to Hungary. They were not given information about the ultimate goal at the beginning of their journey. However, they knew about the agreement made long ago between the Hungarians and the Poles that, in the event of outside aggression against Poland, Hungary would accept its soldiers as refugees. On those grounds, the police officers, now soldiers, were sent there.

The Circuitous Journey toward France

Hungary was far away. The roads were poor, and the transportation was rudimentary. The mountains, forming the border between Poland and Hungary, looked beautiful from a distance. But they made the trip slow and cumbersome. The horses got tired pulling the farm wagons which carried the supplies. The men walked, jumping on the wagon only when they were exhausted. A few personal possessions were allowed. Kaz took his bike, but it was soon lost. He missed it!

The soldiers did not really know where they were going, but they speculated. They slept on the ground in haystacks and were cold at night with no blankets. But everyone was young and there was a feeling of camaraderie. The food was mostly soup, milk, and bread. Occasionally, a scout went on ahead to arrange for cooked food to be prepared for the group.

On their arrival at Komarom, the soldiers discovered that they were not welcome. Expecting to be treated as refugees, they were, instead, treated as prisoners of war. Germany had been gaining rapidly in power.

Hungary was a small nation. Therefore, fear and foreboding of dark times ahead had become commonplace. The Hungarian officials were afraid. The refugees were housed in the barracks vacated by the Hungarian army. A guard was placed at the gate of the compound and at the door of each barrack.

After some time, the Polish men were allowed to go to church, marching in a double line accompanied by a Hungarian guard at the front and another one at the back. "If we wanted to go anywhere, it was always under escort. However, our government-in-exile was soon planning to smuggle us to France, where we'd join the Free Polish Army," Kaz recalled.

After Christmas, in 1939, the Polish government organized its exile government in Paris. The idea was to form an army to fight the Germans along with the French. Some Polish leaders had arrived from Brazil. Some Poles had been living in France. Kaz and his compatriots became part of an ongoing smuggling operation of Polish army personnel from Hungary to France. Documents were falsified. Pictures of the soldiers were attached to these documents and, at church, a few Polish soldiers at a time climbed into the loft during the service. In the loft, they were provided with civilian clothes. They could then leave at the end of the church service to travel toward France, where they planned to join others in fighting the Nazis.

Soon the Hungarian guards began to suspect that something sneaky was going on. Therefore, they started to count the soldiers before they left the barracks for church. However, the soldiers did not let that deter them. As the crew in one barrack was being counted others from a neighboring barrack crept over. The Hungarians could not understand why their count was higher than it was supposed to be. The Poles had some fun with these tricks.

Finally, when it became clear that the numbers were shrinking despite their precautions, the Hungarians put the Poles in an underground fort, which had only one entrance. The fort was outside the city and had been built during the First World War. Without a back door, an escape from it was more difficult.

The only Polish people allowed to visit were the army chaplain and the commanding officer. Attendance at church was now banned. "We were told that we had been bad boys," recalled Kaz. "The living conditions were more than miserable. The bedding consisted of a five-foot board covered by a layer of crumbled and dusty straw. Therefore, it was very unhealthy for breathing. The board was covered with a piece of canvas and a blanket was provided for covering. The food was poor and insufficient."

Kaz was the last one scheduled to emigrate. A week prior to his scheduled leave, the commanding officer brought documents with an address where he should go and directions for how to get there.

Kaz asked, "How are you going to get me out of here? I am a visible person."

"You'll see," was the answer.

The following week, the chaplain and the commanding officer came to visit as was their custom. The commanding officer remarked that Kaz and the chaplain were the same size. The chaplain took off his cape revealing his own captain's uniform. He gave the cape to Kaz.

"How will you get away?" Kaz asked the chaplain.

"That is not your business," the captain answered.

The commanding officer and Kaz, dressed as the chaplain, left the barrack and saluted the guards when outside. On the other side of the fort, a group of men was waiting to give Kaz specific directions.

Kaz was escorted by a civilian man on a train to Budapest. On arrival, he was met by two other men and taken to a place where three other men were waiting for the same expedition. When the group had grown to a dozen or so, they began their journey. They traveled mostly at night on trucks driven by Hungarian drivers. Stopping at daybreak, they were helped by Polish espionage agents who spoke fluent Hungarian. Officially, Poland's relation with Hungary was good now that the Hungarians were also threatened by the Nazis. The Polish soldiers were treated well while they moved toward the Yugoslavian border in the south. The group ended up in Barscazt where the River Drava forms the boundary between the two countries.

A new guide was waiting there to take them across the river in a row boat which held three or four people. This was perhaps at the end of March in 1940. The ice was still floating on the river. On the other side was Yugoslavia where most of the Serbs were not favourably disposed toward the escapees. The Croatians were more cooperative.

On three nights, two to three days apart, the boat tried to take the men across, but turned back when it was clear that the Serbs were on duty. The crossing was dangerous also due to the ice floes which were hard to see in the dark. Added to these dangers, the boats were not in the best of shape. But, eventually, the soldiers did get across and another guide took over.

As they headed toward the Adriatic coast, the unfriendly Serb soldiers were a constant threat. Therefore, it took a long time to cross the country. Finally, the men arrived in Split by the sea. Housed in a resort area a little distance from Split, the group's lodgings were privileged. The men were free to walk to Split, a quite a distance by foot, to buy bananas and other delicacies. The Hungarians had given them money and the Yugoslavians accepted that currency. Kaz enjoyed the holiday feeling of this beautiful area, particularly his leisurely walks on the sandy beach in the warm sunshine.

All too soon, they had to say good-bye to Split and the people they had met. Other Polish soldiers who had arrived earlier joined them on a cargo boat called *Warsaw*. Since the boat was not loaded with a cargo at that time, the weight was not heavy enough for it to stay upright in a fierce storm that blew up between Sicily and Corsica. It was a horrendous journey. It seemed that, at any moment, the boat could tip over and the men would drown. Everyone except the captain was seasick. It was quite a repulsive experience to be among so many people, all throwing up at the same time.

 Making the experience even more horrifying was the fact that the Mediterranean Sea in that area was mined. The boat was in danger of being blown up. The captain sent out an SOS and two Italian destroyers approached. They circled round and round while communicating by Morse code. After a while, they left. Soon afterwards, the winds subsided and the *Warsaw* sailed on.

Very hungry after the storm which had caused seasickness, the men found themselves in Marseilles between two South American cargo boats full of oranges. The sailors threw oranges to the hungry men, who ate so many of them that they became sick – again!

But each one was pleased to be in a free country! This was April, 1940. The soldiers were loaded into a freight train heading for Paris. However, after some time, the train was side tracked and left there for days, in the middle of nowhere. No one dared to go far in case the train started up again. Hungry, Kaz's group searched for food and found a cargo container full of sardine tins packed in oil. The men ate so many sardines that they got sick – AGAIN!

In Occupied France after the No Battle War

Finally, the train arrived near Paris. The men were stationed in the large Polish military camp in Coetguidon. The living conditions were, again, poor. Kaz was billeted in an old horse stall. But, here, the men exchanged their civilian clothes for French uniforms and enjoyed properly cooked food. Their morale was better since they were training and preparing for action against the invaders.

Thousands of young men were being trained at the camp. Many of them had been living and working in the French coal mines before the Nazi invasion of Poland. On his free time, Kaz mingled with them and exchanged memories with the other soldiers who had been able to reach France through Hungary or Romania, or had come from Argentina or Brazil.

The training was basic, learning infantry drills, and communications. The most important task was to get acquainted with the French equipment and weaponry. This was difficult since there was very little ammunition. But, the commanding officers were exceptional teachers. At the end of May, the men finished their training. The Polish units were now somewhat organized. They joined the French army.

Kaz was assigned to reconnaissance work where he was to gain information about the advancing Nazi forces. He used a motorcycle on his surveys to discover the position and movement of the enemy. Marek, eight years Kaz's junior, was working in the same unit. They had become friends during their training. While waiting for their orders, they had time to share memories of their experiences prior to the arrival in France.

Marek was from Warsaw. As a university student, he had been part of the Home Army along with his parents and two sisters. One night, just as he had left the family apartment to deliver a packet of the weekly *Information Bulletin* (a paper printed by the underground press) to their neighbours, a Gestapo unit had marched in and arrested all his family members except a blind aunt and an old servant. Marek heard the commotion and, hiding in the stairway, watched his loved ones being taken away. Helpless, he sat on the stairs and cried while the eerie silence of the curfew descended upon the building.

Marek went back to his home apartment, assured his aunt about the safe return of the family, which he knew was not likely to happen very soon. Previously, before leaving the apartment he had left a briefcase behind the front door. Fortunately, the Gestapo had not noticed the case. He picked it up in order to deliver the hand guns contained in it to other freedom fighters. Then, he left his home.

The next day, *Warsaw* became the target of German bombers. Marek watched the bombs come down in clusters, then explode on tall apartment buildings destroying them and killing hundreds of people. When he saw Gestapo units drag young men into vans, he decided that there was nothing he could do to make things better in Poland at that time.

He knew about the government-in-exile in France and about the possible escape routes out of the country. He decided to travel via Romania. Arranged by the Home Army, he traveled to the border hidden in a haystack on a farmer's wagon. Safe in Romania, he received documents and instructions for his travel to Paris.

Now prepared for combat, Marek's resolve to continue the fight for his homeland was unwavering. At that time, the French army made fortifications to prevent the Nazis from invading Paris from the north. But, the Germans simply went around and entered the city from the south! Also, the Vichy government was shaky in every way. It believed in freedom but did not want to fight for it. Kaz and Marek had been on active duty only a day when the army was gathered together and an announcement was made that the war was over. "Finis la guerre!"

Polish soldiers were disappointed and angry. They did not want to quit so they asked their commanding officer where they could go, next, to fight. Not wanting to abandon them, the officer walked to Paris with them. They ended up late at night outside the city, in the woods, where they stayed in some summer cottages.

Danger was now everywhere because the German army had occupied the surrounding areas. The soldiers learned that, from now on, they could not remain as units. The officer told his men, "I suggest that you form yourselves into groups of two or three and head toward unoccupied France close to the Spanish border. From there, a British boat will take you over to Britain. You are going through a dangerous territory. March at night and stay off the main roads!" He said a general prayer as a blessing, then wished them courage and a successful journey.

But how to achieve that success? The men had no maps of this strange country, no compass, no food, and no way of communicating with anyone. They carried nothing, not even a cup to scoop water. All the bridges were guarded. Swimming across was not a solution because Kaz did not know how to swim! They knew no way of getting help. The French Underground was yet to be born.

Their civilian clothes had been left in Coetguidon. Therefore, everyone wore French uniforms. Kaz and his friend Marek traveled together. Their goal was St. John de Luz, a port city near the French-Spanish border which, along with a small stretch of the western coast and southern France, was still a free country.

Trained as an architect, Marek had also studied engineering intending to combine the two in his career. But, his studies had been interrupted. Earlier, he had been interested in astronomy. On this escape journey, this knowledge proved useful. He knew about the stars and their movements. Trusting that the night sky could show the direction, the pair set out.

Were they afraid? "All the time," Kaz admitted.

There was no way to trust anyone. The Germans patrolled the villages and towns they were to cross. Informants had been bribed already before the invasion. The neighbors watched each other not knowing whom to trust. Kaz had learned while in the police school in Poland that the infiltration takes place before the enemy sets foot on the land.

At times Kaz had serious doubts. But, Marek was encouraging and if an opportunity for collaboration arose, he could communicate since he spoke French. With his positive attitude and sense of humour Marek was a supportive friend. His knowledge of the stars was remarkable—even when they were not all visible due to the clouds covering the sky. They marched at night and slept during the day, often in hay stacks. They stole vegetables and fruits, ate carrots and turnips raw, and cheese that had been hung to dry close to a farmhouse. And they sometimes milked a cow in a hayfield, drinking warm milk directly from its teats. Rain and cloudy skies made trekking at times difficult. Marek's sense of direction never faltered.

The Pair's Capture and the Prisoner of War Camp

Tired and hungry after walking through the night, the pair arrived on a hayfield close to a farm house on the outskirts of a village. Smelling freshly-baked bread, they crept closer. They saw that the loaves had been left to cool near the bake oven in the yard. Seeing no one around, Kaz darted in and picked up a loaf. They were well on their way to the haystacks in the further field when they heard behind them, "Halt!" A German patrol stopped them. They were arrested.

The prisoners were shipped by truck to Germany, just behind the French border, to a temporary holding camp for war prisoners. Kaz and Marek found themselves in a group of French men who were lodged in tents. The area was surrounded by barbed wire.

The treatment of the prisoners was not bad. One day, the German commander gathered them together, and then asked, "Any volunteers to work on a farm?" Marek nudged Kaz and suggested that they volunteer. He whispered, "The food would be better than what we get in this enclave. We'd also have a better chance of escape."

They volunteered and were accepted. They worked hard. The farmer's wife was generous. She fed them well and their sleeping accommodations were good. However, Kaz's friend was patriotic and resolved to free Poland. He reminded Kaz, "Our purpose is not to work for a German farm but to fight for freedom."

Kaz asked, "But where and how?"

"We could march through France and go by boat to England," Marek suggested. "There, we can join the Allied Forces."

A Wehrmacht soldier was in charge of guarding them. They were always under his watchful eye when working. But Marek's plan was simple. "We'll gain his trust and then slip out at an appropriate time that is bound to come."

Luckily, this was not long in coming. It was the early fall of 1940. All the crops were harvested, except potatoes. The nearby village had arranged festivities for the week-end. The whole household went to participate, leaving only the guard to watch the workers. But, the guard had a girlfriend!

Marek and Kaz told the guard that they were content on the farm and that he should go to the village. When the guard returned later that evening to check on them, he saw that they were doing their work.

"How was it?" they asked.

"Oh, it's beautiful!" he exclaimed. "Great dancing and music. Lots of beer!" He laughed.

"Well why don't you go back? We'll be alright and do all the chores. You can come back and check on us. It'll be fine," Marek suggested.

The guard left and stayed away the whole night. Undoubtedly, he was making merry in the village.

Early in the morning, the prisoners did their chores, then put bread, cheese and a few vegetables into a potato sack, which Kaz threw over his shoulder. The pair left to go to unoccupied France. They had been lucky to find civilian clothes in the closet of their assigned room (as if the Frau had intentionally placed them there). This made their travel much easier. A drawing of the main roads and railway lines of France, which they had copied the night before from a map found at the empty house, was in Marek's pocket.

"What if we are caught?" Kaz asked.

"Do not worry! Where there is a will there is a way." Marek answered.

Kaz said, "We'll see."

The Second Journey through the Occupied Zone

While heading southwest, they made connections with the French Underground Army, which, by now, was somewhat organized. Marek communicated in French and they received food and warnings about the possible dangers. They slowly trekked toward the Spanish border. "You may still be able to go over to England," they were told. "If the Nazis have already occupied the coastal area, the Underground Army of France and Spain are cooperating. Go through Spain to Portugal! A boat will take you from there to England."

"Traveling was an unbelievable, dream-like experience. Danger was everywhere, at every step you took. Moving with this uncertainty was nerve-wracking. Every part of the body was taut with tension and ready to spring. You had to have eyes in the back of your head and ears awake when sleeping!" Kaz recalled.

The men acted mechanically. Marek even remarked that he felt numb. The focus in moving from one place to another was that intense. Hunger did not matter as much as the right movements in order to avoid another capture.

One morning, the escapees arrived by a river which they had marked on the now-crumpled map. They wanted to cross that fast-flowing river. Walking further downstream, they saw a rowboat tied to a small tree growing on the bank, then a bridge. On the bridge stood a German guard. He had a gun over his shoulder.

Tired from the night's travel, the pair decided to look for a safe place to sleep. They found it in the bushes higher up. From there they could, after a few hours of sleep, keep an eye on the bridge until dark when they planned to borrow the boat for their crossing. Hungry, they shared a piece of bread which Kaz had saved in his pocket. Throughout the trip, they had never eaten until they were full, always only to satisfy the worst pangs. Hunger was now a natural state. They were occasionally able to save a little bread, knowing that food would not necessarily be waiting at the next stopping place.

At twilight, they crept to the river, away from the view of the bridge. They washed and scooped water into their mouths to satisfy their thirst. Then, they waited for dark. Closer to the boat, they again waited, watching the moving figure on the bridge. When they saw the guard lighting a cigarette and leaning against the rail looking relaxed, Marek whispered, "Now!"

Kaz loosened the rope holding the boat while Marek jumped into it first, then Kaz. Marek pushed it farther from the shore with an oar. Swiftly, the boat drifted downstream. The pair lay low on the bottom and held their breath. Just missing a beam at the side of the bridge, the boat moved far enough out for the men to row it to the other side. The danger had been overcome!

And so they made it through! They arrived in the port city of St. John de Luz just in time. They were last ones to board the boat. It left an hour later toward Britain. They could hardly believe it. They were free! Relieved to be finally out of danger, Kaz and Marek celebrated their freedom on board.

On their arrival in Plymouth, they were directed to a hall where young ladies served them tea and biscuits. They really enjoyed the welcome and, although neither one of them spoke English, they somehow made themselves understood.

Most of the Polish soldiers ended up in Scotland. Many had arrived earlier. Kaz and Marek were delayed because of their hunger and the stolen loaf of bread.

Learning English, Training and Patrolling in Scotland

Heavy fog covered most of England as the train made its way toward Glasgow. Not much of the beautiful country side was visible to the eye. Since Marek and Kaz were still recovering from their adventurous journey in France, they fell asleep at every opportunity. Hearing the announcement, "Glasgow next, Glasgow!" they were surprised to arrive at their destination so soon. They disembarked hurriedly and were met by a Polish soldier who drove them to a Polish camp called 'Bigger'.

In 'Bigger', Marek and Kaz received a royal welcome from the friends who had been part of the same unit in France. Settled in tents and provided with cooked food by the British, the Polish officers and soldiers were trying to get organized and trained. At this point, there was also a great deal of free time.

Marek was interested in seeing the architecture of the Glasgow railroad station. "Would you like to go to see this building with me, Kaz?" he asked.

"Yes, but I don't understand a word of English," Kaz said.

"We'll meet people who speak French and we'll communicate somehow," his friend assured him. A Scottish man took them to the old city. Its architecture was very interesting. Walking for a while, they found themselves close to the railroad station.

Marek had to go to the bathroom. He asked some people in French and in German, where they could find a washroom. No one understood. Finally, Marek took out a piece of paper and wrote two OO's on it. This was the sign for a bathroom in Poland. The man looked at it, went off for a while, and then came back with two prostitutes. "Marek peed in his pants laughing!" said Kaz.

"At the end of the day the question was: Where to stay?" He continued. They sat at a canteen drinking coffee or tea. One of the ladies was able to speak with Marek in French. She made a phone call and a uniformed policeman came in to speak with her.

"Is he going to arrest us?" Kaz asked.

She laughed. "No, but he has an idea of where you can stay."

Marek suggested that they go and see the place. It was some distance away, so they took a streetcar. They arrived near a tall apartment building. Here, they found another lady whose name was Mrs. Steward. She was a ballet teacher who ran a dancing school. She had an extra room, where Kaz and Marek were able to stay.

Mrs. Stewart invited Kaz to come dancing. He wanted to, but hesitated because he did not know English and did not have a dictionary. She did and while enjoying each other's company during the week he stayed there he learned a bit of English. He recalled, "I watched the dancing business, but at her birthday party arranged by her friends I felt like a dummy because I was not able to communicate. I took part in the party to the best of my ability. Everyone was graceful and respectful."

Back at the post, the troops were re-organized. Fresh supplies were needed. Kaz participated in the supply mission. Heavy rain had covered most of northern England for several days. On their return trip, the supply truck was waiting for a Scottish regiment to join them at a fork of two rivers. Suddenly, a river dike broke from the pressure of the water mass. Water began to flood the region. The water surged forcing the men to scamper to higher ground. Most of the supplies and their personal things were swept away. The men were evacuated to Alexandria, a small village nearby.

As the bombings in and around London intensified, information was passed on from the intelligence sources that German paratroopers were to land on the beach near Loch Lomond, Scotland. The Polish contingent was moved to the beach area. Kaz, along with his compatriots, was assigned to patrol the beach. While walking back and forth with a hunting gun over his shoulder, Kaz studied English. He made a list of words he wanted to learn and then spent the day memorizing and learning how to spell them. He met a professional golfer, who later taught him to play the game and invited him to visit his house.

"I need permission from my commanding officer," Kaz said.

"What is his name? I will arrange that."

Kaz spent many evenings learning English with this helpful Scottish gentleman who had three brothers: one in Canada, one in the United States, and one in Australia.

Engrossed in memorizing the text he was reading Kaz nearly collided with a young university student, who was also walking and reading on the beach. A little commotion caused them to get to know each other. They became friends. Invited for dinner by her parents, Kaz enjoyed real English fish and chips and fruit for dessert. For entertainment, his friend played the violin and her mother the piano after the dinner. Kaz has never forgotten the family's kindness and generosity.

With this friendship, Kaz learned more English and improved his pronunciation, which had been a challenge for him. Through the student, he met faculty people at the university including a politics professor who explained to him the difference between capitalism and communism. This knowledge became useful after the war when Kaz had to decide his country of residence. The same professor invited Kaz to visit northern Scotland with him. Remembering the undulating hills and subdued colors he had seen in the foggy countryside, Kaz remarked later, "If the landscape of Scotland was combined with the climate in Canada, Scotland would be the most beautiful country in the world."

The friends who helped Kaz with English did not confuse him by trying to teach him Gaelic. But one expression he remembers from that language is, "Bra necht, Mrs. Recht." (Good night, Mrs. Recht.) Afterwards, the Polish troops were sent to various places. Once in a while, the men had free time. A family at a Bournmouthe's holiday resort welcomed Kaz like their son. He really enjoyed the visits with them.

Correspondence with anyone in Poland was out of the question for Kaz since he had been part of the Polish national forces. Everything would be censored. Even if the letters did not contain anything even vaguely political, his friends or family receiving them could be in trouble with the controlling regime. However, during his free time, Kaz's thoughts wandered back to his family in Poland. He hoped that they were safely 'pocketed' away on the farm, away from the raging war as the Nazi armies advanced toward Moscow. This was not so. He learned that his parents had been taken away from their home. The farm had been left fallow. Their livestock was lost. Fortunately, they were able to return after two years and start all over again.

Kaz's engagement to Valec's sister, Maria, whom he had left with the promise of return, was only a distant memory. While in Scotland, Kaz met a soldier whom he had known while working in the forestry in Poland. From him, Kaz learned that Valec and Maria had also been displaced. They had left the area to an unknown destination sometime in 1942. At that time, displacement was a common practice in occupied Poland.

After leaving Poland, Kaz had experienced one trial after another. First, the travel to Hungary was physically challenging. While living in deplorable conditions in Hungary, his mind was preoccupied with his own escape as he watched his comrades leave one by one. Finally, when his turn came, the journey to France demanded constant adjustment and vigilance. It was not without dangers.

The short training period in France for the 'no battle' war led to an attempt to cross the occupied zone while wearing a French army uniform, traveling at night with no map, no compass, no possible contacts for information, nor food. This, then, resulted in Kaz's and Marek's capture by the Germans. Although the treatment in the prisoner of war camp was not as deplorable as it could have been, they were under constant guard. If the pair was to make their escape, it would require alertness and careful planning.

Their second journey through the hostile terrain meant longer distance than the first one. (It must have been over 1200 km). The Germans had expanded the occupied areas. Their patrols were perfectly organized and stationed in all strategic points. It is almost impossible for us to imagine what it must have been like: to live in constant danger while walking through a strange terrain every night, at dawn being on a look-out for a safe place to sleep, to secure food and water enough to survive, to avoid being seen, shot or captured again. Making it through and 'just' catching the boat to England must have felt like a miracle rescue. And arrival at the Scottish camp must have been an enormous relief.

What was the effect of these ordeals? How had these experiences carrying constant, unpredictable dangers affected Kaz? Or had they? "No," said Kaz, "Of course I was afraid. But, when in danger, you don't analyze. You don't think. You simply do what you have to." He was silent for a moment. Then, he said, "My trust in the Creator has always been strong. I pray. And then, I quietly thank Him when out of danger."

The Allied Forces' Invasion of Normandy

In May, 1940, during the German invasion of France, the British and Allied troops were stationed on Dunkirk beach in northern France. The Germans had succeeded in cutting them off from the other troops and the supply lines. The airfields south of Dunkirk had been overtaken by the Germans and Dunkirk port had come under heavy bombardment. Incredible devastation had followed along the coast of Normandy.

Thirty British naval ships were destroyed. British and French troops, many of their soldiers killed or wounded, were stranded on the beach. Massive losses and evacuation of 400,000 Allied soldiers threw the British into a survival mode. The war was nearly lost. The future of the western way of life hung in balance! During the ten-day rescue operation, all navy ships and hundreds of smaller vessels were employed under heavy aerial fire from the enemy. Many small boats, as well as hundreds of lives, were lost.

However, the troops were rescued. Although Dunkirk had fallen to the enemy, the ten-day Operation Dynamo was deemed a success. Dunkirk was the 'First Front' of the Allied troops. Britain was determined to prepare for the 'Second Front' in which the rescued troops would form the core of the army.

At this crucial time in history, when the Nazi forces were advancing in all parts of the globe, Winston Churchill emerged as the leader and Prime Minister of England. He said, "Now this is not the end. It is not even the beginning of the end. But it is, perhaps, the end of the beginning." The Western nations were stirred into action by his originality, his awe-inspiring resolve, and his humour. He believed in the final victory. Because of this, ordinary people believed and developed trust, essential for any undertaking.

His amazing optimism carried the English through the bombings, through the loss of life, through rationing of the essentials and hunger. His brilliant commitment aroused young men and women to join the fight for freedom.

But, however noble Churchill's ideas and optimism were, he had his faults. Impulsiveness, even recklessness, led him to send troops to fight in situations leading to further losses in Normandy, Greece, Singapore, and Tobruk. Churchill was not a strategist. The offensives he ordered cost thousands in military personnel, ships, and aircraft, "All thanks to a triumph of impulse over a reason," as Max Hastings stated in his book, *Winston's War*.

A towering figure in modern history, Winston Churchill's unflinching optimism with his sayings such as, "Attitude is a little thing that makes a big difference," galvanized the western world into action against the ruthless machinations of the Nazis.

His exhilarating speeches were communicated frequently through the radio to millions in the military as well as in civilian life. The speeches mesmerized everyone. Kaz had vivid memories of Churchill's poignant sayings that built trust in the soldiers preparing to enter into action. To those already on the battlefield, Churchill said, "I have nothing to offer but blood, toil, tears, and sweat," and, "If you are going through hell, keep going!"

The trust Winston Churchill had in the guidance of the Almighty, which he shared in his inimitable way, reached every heart. He must also have recognized his own limitations in war planning and strategy for he said, "Really, I feel less keen about the Army every day. I think the Church would suit me better." According to the way he was able to inspire and build trust, his role was, indeed, more of a priestly nature than that of a secular leader.

Many Polish soldiers who first arrived in Scotland had armoured experience. A small unit was set up to reflect this. Kaz joined this quickly-expanding Polish 1st Armoured Division which was formed as a part of the First Polish Corps. It guarded approximately 200 kilometres of the British coast.

Kaz was sent to several training centres, including Bovington in southern England, where he became familiar with vehicles used in the war. He learned to drive tanks, trucks and motorcycles of different types. During the Bovington course, he learned how to do minor tank repairs and how to detect an approaching enemy aircraft.

He learned everything he needed to know about the Sherman tanks. This would become his operational vehicle when entering into action. Sherman, named after a Civil War hero, was the classic American tank used by all Allied forces during the Second World War. It was not one of the best tanks. It was inferior to some of the Soviet and German tanks in armour and firepower. Because of this, it gained the nickname "The

Tommycooker". It was simple, rugged, easy-to-fix and quite fast for its time with a top speed of 38km/h.

The British version was called the Firefly. It had a powerful seventeen-pd gun. The largest of the guns in each tank was mounted to the revolving turret which was usually manned by the tank commander, the radio operator, and the first gunner. Each one of the tank crew was taught how to fire guns. The cramped quarters within the tank required precise skill and co-operation from the members of the crew. Therefore, a good part of the training was spent practising working together within the tank. During the training, many disagreements arose amongst the men. However, many friendships, lasting throughout the war even a lifetime, were also forged.

Forced laughter and tough expressions hid the feelings of the young men. No one wanted to appear weak and afraid of what laid ahead. Humor was created from incidents that happened within each unit. In one incident, a unit was inspected by a sergeant major. He stopped in front of a private and looking at his boots said, "Dirty! You want me to clean your boots?"

The private stammered, "Yes, sir."

"Yes?" repeated the sergeant major.

"Yes, sir. No, sir," stammered the private.

The snap saying: "Yes Sir. No Sir!" was widely repeated for months afterwards.

Field-Marshal Montgomery and his troops returned from the North African campaign bringing with them their experience and techniques.

While mingling with these officers and soldiers, the others learned the way things worked in action and the kind of discipline it required. When Montgomery assigned troops for the British operation, it was suggested that Kaz take a course in using compasses since they were used to navigate in Africa. He did that. Generally, Kaz spent as much time as possible in training himself. Eventually, he became an instructor.

Later, a group of sergeants was selected to look after the needs of the officers who had returned from Africa and were re-training for the operation in Europe. Kaz was delegated to be one of the sergeants. He recalled, "We were billeted together. When we went to the shooting range, we saw officers with white gloves and sticks under their arms. To us, this was really funny.

But, they obeyed because that was Montgomery's order."

According to Kaz the Marshal was ruthless, clever, and proud. He had little sympathy for anyone's weaknesses. He expected from others the same discipline he practised himself. But, he did have some sense of humor according to a story concerning an American journalist, who came to the British compound to interview him. Asking to see him, the newspaper man was pointed toward a tent some distance away. On his way, he met Montgomery but did not recognize him. When asked where he could find Montgomery, the Marshal pointed toward his tent. On arrival, the journalist asked the Marshal's private secretary, with a reserved tone of respect, if he could interview him.

Uncompromisingly, Marshal Montgomery focused on success and persisted with his ideas. A dispute regarding tactics arose between him and Eisenhower, then the commander of the United States forces. Knowing that the Germans were prepared for a second front in Europe, Eisenhower wanted the offensive to take place in Yugoslavia, behind the German lines. Montgomery's plan prevailed and the Second Front was opened in Europe with the invasion on D-Day.

Field-Marshal Montgomery said to his troops on the eve of D-Day, "With stout hearts and with enthusiasm for the contest, let us go forward to victory!" The largest land/water invasion in human history was to take place on June 4th 1944 on the fifty-mile stretch of the Normandy coast in France. Because of the weather conditions the landing was delayed two days. On the morning of June 6th, five thousand ships were involved in disembarking heavy and light artillery, tanks, trucks and over 140,000 Allied soldiers.

Marshal Montgomery had re-organized the army. Kaz recalled, "He spoke to the whole division and said that they were going to employ a special weapon to boost the progress in France. The commanding officer who was next to him asked, 'Say Sir, can we ask what this secret weapon is?'

"'It is the Polish 1st Armoured Division!' Montgomery answered. I think he said it to boost our morale, but that is how our group got involved in the battles."

Kaz continued, "When the Canadians came to England, they were supposed to join the British. But, right from the beginning, they did not like the food, the uniform, the discipline. They went back to Ottawa. 'We'll organize our own army!' Prime Minister King stated. He had quite a job to have this matter put to the parliament and when the decision was made he sent General Grerer from Canada, a very nice man, to be in charge of the Canadian forces.

"Due to the circumstances involving Montgomery's scheme, the Canadians were short of armoured brigades. For that reason, the Polish division became a part of the Canadian army. On our tanks, above their number 52, two letters were added – PL for Poland. (Grant Harper, a veteran and a resident at Hesperus, tells me that he saw some of those tanks when he was fighting). Earlier, the Polish 1st Armoured Division was created as an independent unit. It was in 1944 that it became a part of the Canadian army.

"London was bombed frequently, at that time. While visiting it, during one of the blitzes, we saw the sky full of balloons. 'Why so many balloons?' we asked an Englishman."

"'So many foreigners have recently arrived that we need the balloons to keep the country afloat,' was his answer. The real reason, of course, was that balloons prevented the enemy planes from flying low enough to bomb their targets. Balloons hitting the engines would have crashed the planes."

When the D-Day invasion took place in Normandy, Kaz was not with his regiment but doing his job in the centre for retraining officers. Marshal Montgomery wanted to retrain all the officers, including the generals, and also some from the non-commissioned ranks. Kaz looked after the re-trainees' needs. His job was to keep them informed about their new assignments, and to act as a liaison when something was needed or was not working according to needs in their living quarters or in the dining room. When asked whether he liked the job, Kaz answered, "In the army you like what they tell you to do. Otherwise, you end up being endlessly miserable."

Since he had training in driving tanks and there was a shortage of tank commanders Kaz was pulled out of his job. In order to report for duty, he headed for London. Later he joined his unit in France.

"We didn't go over in the first waves at D-Day but were sent over several weeks later. Montgomery held us as a secret weapon, a tag he used to boost our morale."

Dnia 7. VIII. 44. wieczorem długi sznur czołgów wypełznął na drogi.
On the evening of the 7-th of August long line of tanks drew up on the road.

Morale boosting has always been an important part of war. Soldiers have to endure long periods of waiting during the preparations. Not all of them are eager volunteers. Many are conscripted to the army for the country's survival. In many cases, the men are already gripped by fear which they cannot share with anyone or shake off during training.

Someone has to reawaken their fervour and lift up their spirits. But in the earlier centuries, the king or whoever fought against the neighboring state was at the front of his army to give an example of his own bravery.

In contrast, the present-day leaders are not seen on the battlefield. They are strategic planners in the war office. For instance, Stalin, the ruthless leader of the Soviet Union for decades, directed his military campaigns from Moscow. That way it must have been easier for him to say, "Death of one person is a tragedy; death of a million is statistics!"

Nowadays, in order to boost the fighters' morale, the leader appears in front of his army before it is led to action. He emphasizes his soldiers' special talents and strong fighting spirit and with a military march to follow they are directed to a battle, many to the final days of their lives.

As a Tank Commander in the Bloody Battle of Falaise Gap

The Battle of Falaise, or Falaise Gap, received its name from the series of operations in which a large number of German Wehrmacht and SS divisions were trapped in the Falaise Pocket and, subsequently, destroyed during the Normandy campaign (the Second Front) in the summer of 1944.

General Maczek's Polish division had the crucial role of closing the pocket at the escape route of the German divisions. The fighting was absolutely desperate. The Polish 1st Armoured Division, supported by the Infantry Battalions, took the brunt of the attacking Germans who were trying to break free from the pocket. The Polish Division withstood incessant attacks from multiple fleeing German armoured divisions.

In this bloody campaign, Kaz was a troop commander in 2nd Squadron of the Polish 1st Armoured Division. He was responsible for three tanks, fifteen men and equipment. Each tank had a leader, a radio operator, and a gunner stationed in the turret, and a driver and a machine gun operator stationed below. Of course, in addition to being a troop commander, he was the leader of his tank which had a seventeen-pound gun in the turret. There were three tanks in a troop, four troops in a squadron, three squadrons in a battalion, and a special troop for the top commanding officer who had two tanks under his direct command.

The Polish Armoured Division was a part of the Canadian army, semi-independent of British control, although Marshal Montgomery was the General of all the Western Allied Forces. The Polish division, led by popular General Maczek, was a key part of the Canadian armoured capacity. The Polish troops were with the Canadian contingent until the end of the war.

Kaz recalled, "I rejoined the Polish Division in Caen, France. At that time, we had a little break. This gave us opportunities for discussions. Most of my crew members were Polish. The feeling within the group was like family. We felt that, since we were in this together, we must work in unison, take care of each other in tight spots. Before going into action, we asked ourselves: 'What does it mean to kill? Are we not responsible for everything we do whether in civilian life or in war situation?'

"Finally, in one of our discussions, we decided that we would not kill—at least directly. We planned to maneuver our movements as a unit in subtle ways, with an infantry unit always close by, often traveling on top of our tanks. When in a battle, my gunners did not shoot directly to kill the enemy, but shot overhead. Instinctively, the enemy soldiers threw themselves on the ground. The infantry unit moved swiftly to take them as prisoners. I told my boys to keep quiet about this. Each one understood that, if our practice was known, we would be court martialed, possibly shot. Those were the rules of war! However, no one ever complained to me about the fact that we took prisoners. During my six-year war experience I did not kill and I did not get killed. There must be something in that for future generations!

"I lost some of my hearing due to sticking my head out of the turret. The periscopes we had at our disposal did not give us a good enough view of the situation. So, at times, we would risk our lives by putting our heads out of the turret. Several commanders were lost this way because the helmets were not strong. Bullets could go right through them. Also, the helmets did not cover our ears. They were designed in this manner so that we could hear the two-way radios we used for communication. We used one frequency to communicate within our troop of three tanks and another frequency (which changed daily) to communicate with our superiors.

"We soon experienced real hell. Falaise-Gap was hell, believe me! Every tank commander had a possibility of radio communication with the commanding officer of the unit, but there was little in the way of organized fighting.

"On the radio, 'Go! Go! Go forward! Go! Go!' a voice shouted constantly in our ears. On our left, a tank was burning; on our right, a tank was burning. Who was going to be next? The fighting went on, day and night. Everything was so mixed up. It wasn't even funny! You didn't know against whom you were fighting.

"It took three days of staring death in the face. I can't remember. We did not sleep. The emergency rations had run out in the first twenty-four hours. The water container was low and we were scared stiff.

"Suddenly my first gunner became hysterical. He cried, 'I have to get out!'

"He closed the bar in the turret which kept me protected when the gun re-tracked upon firing. He reached up to open the top latch in order to get out. I dragged him down. He collapsed, whimpering, and then got on to his knees to pray. I kicked him in the ass and said, 'Too late for that now. Get up and do your job!'

"He got up, disengaged the bar he had closed, and set up to aim. 'You should have done your praying before this mess,' I added. His eyes wild with fear, he turned the gun from side to side without finding a target. 'Breathe in and find a target,' I yelled.

"Sweat pouring down my face made my mouth taste salty. It was hot. The noise of explosions was deafening. The air was filled with smoke. The wheat fields, which had been almost ready for harvesting, were burning fast. Tree stumps were smoldering and black. Across the field, a house was on fire. No one was there to stop it. On the side of the road, a dog was running in circles barking in fear. The crew inside the tank moved as if they were mesmerized, doing their job mechanically, while the voice on the radio repeated its call, urging us to advance. There was nothing else to do but to try to go forward. When would it stop? What if we were hit?" Kaz wondered.

It was scary and unpredictable. At first, air support was sporadic. This was a problem as the Allies' tanks could only damage German armour within a mile while the Germans could destroy their enemy at a range of two miles. The American-made Sherman tanks were made of soft metal. Therefore, a bullet could go in one side and come out from the other side. However, the softer metal had one advantage: when it was hit, the crew didn't have to face as many splinters as they must have in the enemy tanks. At Falaise Gap, Kaz lost one tank and two crewmen.

Kaz recalled another mishap, "The air force had the exact location of where to bomb. But, on the ground, things changed rapidly. In one particular instance, a bomb was dropped on our own forces. The infantry lost many people. Luckily, we did not lose anyone. After that, changes were made."

Sprawdzanie sieci radiowej.
Testing the wireless set.

Soon, a dependable air support was in place, operating under a firm procedure. The commanding officer would be informed of the enemy position, the details of which he would forward to air force control. Ground attack aircraft would approach while the armoured unit fired a smoke grenade to indicate the location of the enemy. The planes would then take care of the threat. This way, no accidents could happen.

The area in which the pocket had formed was full of the remains of the battle. Whole villages had been destroyed, ruined. Abandoned equipment made some roads totally impassable. Corpses littered the area – not only those of the soldiers but also civilians and thousands of dead cattle and horses. In the hot weather, maggots crawled over the bodies and hordes of flies descended on the area. Pilots reported being able to smell the stench of the battlefield from hundreds of feet above it.

General Eisenhower recorded," The battlefield at Falaise was, unquestionably, one of the greatest 'killing fields' of any of the war areas. Forty-eight hours after the closing of the gap, I was conducted through it on foot, to encounter scenes that could be described only by Dante. It was, literally, possible to walk for hundreds of yards at a time stepping on nothing but dead and decaying flesh."

And Kaz recalled, "Falaise was declared out of bounds due to the dead soldiers and animals, which had begun to rot. The stink was unbearable. Special units came solely to bury the dead."

The men were tired, tired from lack of sleep and from all the stress, which terror, and a life-and-death struggle brings, with its desperate need for alertness. A deadening explosion could destroy the unit in one blast. They had seen plenty of such examples in the past few days. As his body began to slump and his eyes wanted to close, Kaz reminded himself of General Patton's advice. The general noted, "Now, if you are going to win any battle you have to do one thing. You have to make the mind run the body. Never let the body tell the mind what to do. The body will always give up. It is always tired morning, noon, and night. But the body is never tired if the mind is not tired. When you were younger, the mind could make you dance all night, and the body was never tired. . . You've always got to make the mind take over and keep going."

The Canadian/Polish forces had succeeded in Falaise. They had to regroup. Some of the men were delegated to the reinforcing unit which was responsible for transportation of equipment from the ports. The equipment had been greased to protect it from salt which had accumulated during the sea voyage. This grease had to be removed. Since this unit was short-handed, Kaz's group was delegated to help.

Kaz recalled, "A funny incident happened while we were working at the reinforcing unit. The Canadians were called off by name not by rank. One day, on the field, an English officer came in to pick up equipment. 'Where is the officer's mess?' he asked.

"'We don't have one. If you want a meal, line up like the rest of the boys!' he was told.

Kaz's expression changed when he continued, "But I also witnessed a more serious incident, an example of the cruelty of war. At the same army base, the German prisoners were lined up in a single file. An Allied officer moved from one prisoner to the next asking each his name, the number of his regiment, and the name of a close relative who was to be informed about his imprisonment. These questions were part of the international rules on how the prisoners of war were to be treated and how they, in turn, were to respond. The questions were to be answered and every soldier knew it.

"The officer came to ask a German soldier. He was possibly a member of the feared SSTotenkopt unit, trained to kill and brainwashed as a 'Hitler Jugend' to hate all foreigners. When the officer asked the question, the young man spit on his face and threw his head backwards in defiance. The officer, without a flinch, took a few steps backwards, pulled out his revolver, and shot the young man. He then said loudly, in German, 'Let this be a lesson to you all.' Then, he continued his interrogation.

Thirteen Hundred and Fifty Eight Kilometres of War

In less than two weeks, Kaz was back at his regiment. At that time, they were still in France. There was not much fighting until the troops got through Belgium to Holland. On the march to Belgium, something happened to Kaz's tank. It would not move and there was no radio response.

Szybko zbudowano trochę ciasne, ale bezpieczne „mieszkanie".
Not much room to sleep in, but safety comes first.

The men dug out a sleeping place under the tank for protection, and settled in to spend the night. They had used up their reserve rations and were getting hungry. The gunner, who had gone out to make contact, met a Canadian rescue unit. On his return, he explained that the unit's radio communicated only with their own commanding officer and, therefore, the rescue unit was not able to make contact with Kaz and his men. They were assumed dead. (This was one of the two times that Kaz was considered to be dead during the war). After a week, they were rescued. The regiment had quite a celebration upon their return. Kaz was given another tank.

After Falaise and during the Allies' push towards Belgium and, then Holland, the Germans struggled with limited supplies of petrol. The Allied troops would often pass by their abandoned trucks and armoured vehicles on the roads. The enemy's goal was now to delay the Allies as much as possible. Often they would wire up mines and bombs under the road, which they could explode as a tank passed over it. But, the tension was too great for those who set off the charge. Many mines exploded prematurely.

By the time the troops arrived in Belgium, Kaz's whole crew was Polish, but could speak English which many of the Belgians spoke. The soldiers stayed in their country for several weeks. They were entertained with food and wine and they had free time to get to know people while sitting on park benches watching children at play. Kaz does not remember the name of the place. But he does remember how beautiful it was in the sunshine.

Po bitwie.
When the battle was over.

Kaz met a kind tailor who offered to make him a suit. Not knowing when he would have an opportunity to wear it, he asked the tailor, who answered, "When you are out of the army!"

"That was pleasing to hear," said Kaz. "So I agreed and he made me a fine suit, which I, unfortunately, had to crumple up in my knapsack with all my other belongings. He was a fine tailor."

On their way to Holland, the troop was caught in a battle, where a barrel of Kaz's big gun was hit by a bullet. The barrel became dented and they were unable to use the gun. He radioed his superiors asking for someone to come and fix it. The area was known to be mined and he did not receive a response. No repair men were willing to risk their lives crossing the mine field. After a day, Kaz's friend, Ted, whom he had known since their time together in Scotland, appeared. He had managed to drive through the field unharmed. He made the gun operational in no time. Ted had been a professional soldier in Poland and while in England he had been trained to fix all kinds of equipment.

The fighting wasn't as intense as it had been in Normandy, although none of the soldiers expected the war to end soon. The Polish 1st Armoured Division pursued the Germans and liberated, among others, the towns of Saint Omer, Ypres, Ghent, and Passhendaele. American and Canadian units were working in the same area. On approaching Holland, the Polish Division was directed toward Breda.

Przemówienie Dowódcy Korpusu do Oficerów.
The General spoke to the Officers.

A successful maneuver to get around and behind the enemy force was planned and performed by General Maczek. This allowed the liberation of Breda on October 29, 1944. Kaz recalled, "Pushing into the Netherlands, one of the most memorable occasions was the liberation of a town called Breda, where we were royally welcomed. On gathering information, we learned that a local church was still in the German hands and sharpshooters were trying to shoot civilians from the steeple. I said to one of my tank leaders, 'Flush them out and get a bunch of prisoners from there!' My men shot into the church and the German soldiers came out with their hands up. They were taken to a holding unit within the city, later to be sent to a prisoner of war camp. They could no longer bother the citizenry."

The soldiers of the Polish 1st Armoured Division were hailed as the liberators of the city. Dutch people, in their appreciation, were very expressive. The men were thronged and cheered by people of all ages. Young girls crowded around the tanks and expressed their gratitude by decorating them with spontaneous artworks. The Mayor of Breda gave a welcome speech to the liberators and General Maczek was later made an honorary citizen of the town.

The Division spent the winter of 1944-45 on the south bank of the River Rhine guarding a sector around Moerdijk, Netherlands. Kaz recalled, "We were there quite a long time while the Germans were withdrawing along the coastline." Orders came to stop the Germans' withdrawal at Moerdijk. The units were not told why they were to do that. Perhaps it was to pocket the enemy the way it had been done in Falaise. In order to get to their Moerdijk area position, the tanks had to cross an important canal flowing east. The commanders had been told that the infantry was already over the canal at Moerdijk, holding a position for the tanks.

Uszkodzone i zniszczone mosty wymagały wiele materiału do naprawy.
Repair of damaged and destroyed bridges took huge quantities of material.

How the German tanks were positioned on the other side was not totally clear to the commanders of Kaz's squadron. But, the Canadian engineers built a bridge at a certain crossing point. As soon as the bridge was built, the German's tank fire blew it up. This happened twice while the tanks waited to get across. There must have been a spy, perhaps a paratrooper, who had integrated himself earlier into the Dutch population. He may have had access to the information of the Allied Forces' exact locations as well as their maneuvers.

Finally, it was decided that the tanks were to cross the canal on a makeshift pontoon. It was built by erecting a wooden platform between two boats. This was a dangerous operation. Each tank driver had to use his best skill to place the tank on the platform floating on water. Entering the wrong way could easily upset the whole rickety construction. At two in the morning, the first tank was on the platform and was pontooned to the other side. In the dead of night, each one was ferried across.

At dawn, the men realized that they were covered in a thick fog, "You could not see your out stretched hand," said Kaz. The tanks were lined up along a road with deep ditches on both sides. They waited for the fog to lift. As it cleared, they found themselves two feet above a swampy field with no trees or bushes anywhere to be seen. They were an easy target for the enemy fire that could have been shot from a distance of two miles and still penetrate a tank.

Explosions were deafening: they happened in front, back and on both sides. Kaz could see tanks on fire in front of his. "We were just sitting there like ducks," said Kaz. "Never before, in my whole army life, had I seen such gunfire!"

Kaz shouted to his drivers through the two-way radio, "Don't give them a target! Move back and forth!" He stood in the turret in order to have a better view of the situation. (He had discovered a long time before this that the periscopes were useless).

Jeden z naszych zniszczonych czołgów.
One of our tanks knocked out.

Suddenly he felt it! The tank shook from the impact. He looked down and realized that a bullet had come in from the right side of the tank and gone through the other side. The vertical pole supporting his seat had been hit. The bullet missed his legs by two inches. The tank was on fire! Kaz cried to his men, "Jump out!"

They were already in the deep ditch by the road when Alex, the driver, grabbed a handle on the tank, and pulled himself back as he cried, "I forgot the whiskey!" Luckily, he was back in the ditch before the gas stored below the turret exploded.

"Alex was a brave man!" recalled Kaz. "That whiskey kept us warm as we crawled along the ditch looking for a suitable crossing back to the Allied territory. After several attempts to contact the infantry using the radio, we finally succeeded and learned that a cable had been secured at a certain point for crossing to the other side."

All eighteen tanks were destroyed by the enemy fire. By the end of that day, they were burned to skeletons. Miraculously, there was no loss of personnel. At the crossing point, some men swam while others waded, neck-deep in water, to the other side by using their hands and the cable stretched across the canal. All ninety men were safe, but shivering from the November cold. They were tired and hungry.

Kaz went to the mess hall located in a large private house. He did not want to eat. He felt as if a cold was coming on. A chaplain walked into the room, looked at him up and down and said, "You don't look well. Go to the kitchen and ask for a mug of rum. Cover yourself and sip the rum."

So Kaz did that. He went to the place where he was billeted, sat in bed to sip the rum, and then went to sleep. "Next day I felt like a newborn," said Kaz. "It was naval rum, Black Label."

The period that followed was full of tedious waiting. Kaz and his comrades used this time to get to know the locals. Since most of the people they met spoke English communication in English provided good practice for the men who often used their native Polish while they were amongst each other.

The tanks had been destroyed. New ones had to be shipped from Antwerp where they had been stored after their arrival from the United States. Finally, when the troops received the tanks, they were cleared of the grease and equipped with guns, ammunition, gas, and

Gotów do akcji.
Ready for action.

emergency rations. Then they were ready for action.

Snow was already on the ground when the commanders received a communication that German paratroopers were expected to land around the airport in Breda. It was nearly Christmas. This alerted everyone because of the reports that, the previous year, a

German commando unit had interrupted Christmas Eve celebrations of a company and taken everyone as prisoners.

Breda needed protection and Kaz's troops were assigned to do that. Nothing happened. The skies were clear. No enemy planes carrying paratroopers were detected. Forced to stay in or around their tanks parked in bushes close to the snowy air field, Kaz and his crew celebrated Christmas and welcomed the year 1945 while on tedious duty in the cold. Christmas dinner was a box delivered to the tanks. It had an extra piece of ham, mashed potatoes, and peas. Unfortunately, due to the transportation, it was not exactly a hot dinner. The dessert was vanilla pudding.

"Not much of a Christmas! When is this war going to end?" The men asked, some quite bitterly. Stressed and cold in spite of the overcoats and sweaters they wore, many smoked or rolled cigarettes while they recalled and shared their life experiences. But only a little of Christmas memories was expressed, for sharing feelings was a taboo. No one wanted to give the impression of being weak or sissy. What was in each heart was kept locked within, the way it had been throughout the winning and losing battles of the war.

Five months of action had changed everyone. Does anyone ever feel ready for a battle? Yes, perhaps a young man can think he is ready while imagining its dangers. And that's how many volunteers, young and inexperienced, end up on the battlefield.

The Falaise-Gap experience in France had been a baptism to the realities of war. But, danger had also been constant during the thirteen hundred and fifty eight kilometers which the Canadian regiment, including the Polish Armoured Division, had traveled while liberating Belgium and then Holland.

During every move, a sniper with a machine gun could be hiding around the corner. A mine could blow up the tank, the way it had happened to one with eight infantry men riding on top of it.

A bomb, hidden under the roadway, had exploded. The tank was thrown thirty metres or so. The men inside were tossed about and bruised, but alive. The ones on top had been mutilated so badly by the explosion that not one body could be identified.

Nareszcie można zjeść coś z kuchni.
A hot meal at last.

Each tank was supplied with the rations to be used in emergencies. But they also became handy when the troops had to wait for days while a reconnaissance unit was investigating the territory for massive road blocks, blown-up bridges, or for enemy units hiding in towns. The rations, consisting of dry bread and concentrated protein, were, of course, not very appetizing. However, they came in really handy when the tanks were able to stop by a farm.

Alex, carrying the rations, went to negotiate with the farmer. Invariably, he came back with two or three chickens, potatoes, and sometimes apples. The second gunner, Mark, was a great cook. He carried, in his knapsack, pouches of salt, pepper and herbs that enriched the flavor of every meal he prepared in the little stove which was a part of the tank equipment. When the meat was cooked by Mark, the meal surpassed any other one the men had ever had. "Hunger is the best cook!" Kaz noted. "But hunger with a good cook is even better."

The plan was to move slowly onward. But winter soon set in and the general advance came to a halt. The tanks now patrolled designated areas, supporting the infantry near River Maas which had to be closely watched because of the threat of German infiltration. The regiment remained in Holland until the spring of 1945.

The armoured units were stationed in the beautiful city of 's-Hertogenbosch, located by the Maas, a branch of the Rhine in southern Holland. The city was conquered by the Germans in 1940 and was liberated in the fall of 1944 by the British 53rd (Welsh) Division. The area has a long history of suffering and conflicts. One of the few official concentration camps in western Europe located outside of Germany and Austria, was named after 's-Hertogenbosch. The camp complex operated from January 1943 to September 1944. About 30,000 inmates were interned in the camp during this time. About 12,000 of them were Jewish. In the Netherlands, the camp was known as Kamp Vught because it was located on a heath near Vught, a village a few kilometres south of 's-Hertogenbosch. It was a tragic coincidence that the entire Jewish population of 's-

Hertogenbosch had been burned alive on the same heath in the thirteenth century.

In January 1945, the Polish tank troops were transferred to this area. Groups of Germans used to cross the frozen river to set off bombs and blow up bridges. It was not only soldiers that came. German civilians, also, were known to cross the river to rob farms and people. Hunger was everywhere. Natives of Holland were hungry. The Germans across the border were hungrier still.

Infantry troops patrolling the shores were not able to handle the influx of attacks. The tanks were needed as an efficient deterrent. They were stationed in strategic positions, chosen based on the information given by Dutch informants. When Germans were expected to cross, a machine gun fire was directed to the crossing point to prevent the intrusion. Sometimes, the information was not received. When a German group was already crossing the river, the tank's machine gun operator shot above or around the group, who instinctively threw themselves on the ice. The infantry moved in quickly to take them as prisoners.

After five months of active campaign, Canadian and Polish soldiers were now experienced warriors. But, the wintering by the Maas was no party for they had to keep the Germans on their toes.

While American and British armies launched attacks farther south, the infantry and tanks had to give the enemy the impression that an assault was imminent. This was done to force the Germans to leave troops in that area. In all areas, the Allied Forces patrolled in an aggressive way, using every opportunity to gain some ground or take a prisoner.

The duty on River Mass was two weeks on two weeks off. For the Polish platoon, that meant three tanks for every two weeks. Spring came early in 1945. When the ice on the river melted, the men practised sports, including fishing, in their free time. This period left strong, pleasant memories in the minds of the exhausted men.

The soldiers had gone through hell. They had seen many killed. They had encountered dead bodies lying on a roadside. They had heard the wounded cry in agony before they received relief and were removed from the battlefield. They had seen others collapse from battle exhaustion or become hysterical under the stress of ever-present death. They had faced mortars, shells, and bullets every day. And, they had witnessed other soldiers being taken prisoners by the Germans.

Now, sitting on the river bank in the warm sun, holding a fishing rod and letting bare feet hang as the river current caressed them was an enormous relief to the men. In no time, the bucket sitting beside them was filled with trout, pike, and other fish.

Kaz and his men were billeted in a private residence housing a family who had escaped from Amsterdam. They had three children: two boys and a girl. The father had been an insurance agent in Amsterdam and the mother was a good cook. She was happy to prepare the bounty of fish.

The family shared what they had and provided their visitors with as much of a family life as was possible under the circumstances. During the breaks, the men fraternized with many other Dutch people. They walked and talked, and told stories, speaking English.

The Last Explosion

Germany had been fighting losing battles on both fronts, against the Russians in the east and against the Allied Forces in the west. At some point, the Allied Forces managed to cut all supply lines to the German troops. That meant no ammunition, and no food. The German's resistance weakened day by day. There were no attacks from their air or ground troops. "The whole German army was very weak. They did not put up any fight. But they used to delay action by burying bombs, then pressing the trigger when a tank was over the bomb," recalled Kaz.

The armoured units received an order from headquarters to travel on the highway north toward the naval port of Wilhemshaven, in Germany. The tanks had to pass through a section where enemy snipers were reportedly shooting from the bushes. There was no infantry to provide protection for the tanks. The tank commanders had orders to fire into any suspicious looking places. So that is what they did on both sides of the road.

Kaz recalled, "The march was slow. We had to be careful not to lose any personnel or equipment. But, in early May, 1945, we were in Germany. On one particular day, it was my turn to be in the front. We would alternate. The person in the front tank was the eyes and the ears of the unit. I told my driver to go slowly. I was looking through my binoculars standing in my turret. I knew, from the map, that we were about to cross a railroad track, so I was watching. Then I saw a vision! The railroad track was lifting up. We were about a hundred feet from it!

"We came closer. The Jerries had buried a bomb under the railroad track, but it had exploded before we got there. The bomb created a hole big enough for a house."

The rain was heavy and there was water on both sides of the road, making it impossible for the tanks to maneuver on the marshy ground. This was in the afternoon. Canadian engineers were called in to check the crater and to rebuild. The men set up camp at dusk and were waiting in a tent when a Canadian sergeant came in. "Wonderful news! Tomorrow at eight o'clock, the war will end."

"You must be kidding!" Kaz remarked.

"'No! It's an official order from Montgomery's headquarters," replied the sergeant.

Kaz smiled as he recalled, "This was May 5, 1945. We couldn't believe it, at first. Then there was no end to our excitement. We celebrated and could not sleep, waiting with baited breath.

"The next morning, dead on at eight o'clock, there was nothing but silence," Kaz remembered, "You couldn't hear a shot anywhere. It was an amazing feeling. Sitting in front of our tent with coffee mugs in our hands, it was as if time had stopped. No-one spoke. Each one was buried in his own thoughts and feelings for a long time."

Msza Święta.
Holy Mass.

Witnessing Devastation

A liaison officer from the German army was to come and lead the Allied troops to Wilhemshaven, the largest German naval base in the north. The troops were told that the German officer would be carrying a white flag. Everyone was excited. Kaz recalled, "The officer came in a Jeep. The flag was like half a bed sheet fastened to a pole beside the driver. He wanted to make sure that everyone on route could see it.

"We followed him to Wilhemshaven. I am not sure what time we entered. It was only twenty-five kilometres. But the march was slow for the forty-eight tanks. On the way, we saw many German soldiers and low-ranking officers sitting, looking broken down and exhausted on the side of the road. Seeing the white flag in front of our retinue, they simply sat downcast. It must have been close to evening when we arrived.

Dochodzimy do Wilhelmshaven.
We came nearer and nearer Wilhelmshaven.

"What we saw when we entered Wilhelmhaven was something phenomenal. We saw German troops surrendering by raising their hands. When we entered onto the main street the tracks were so deep that the belly of the tank was dragging on the ground. The whole infrastructure of the city was damaged. The underground was full of water.

"We went to the German naval barracks and settled there. It had a big gate with our guards standing in front of it. Children at first gaped from a distance. Slowly, they dared to come closer. The German population had been told that the enemies would kill them. Instead, they received candy from our guards."

On May 6, General Maczek of the Polish division accepted the surrender of the Kriegsmarine naval base, of the entire garrison including some two hundred ships and more than ten infantry divisions. There, the division ended the war and was replaced by the Polish First Independent Parachute Brigade, which undertook occupation duties until 1947 when the division was disbanded. Kaz concluded, "I don't think that we stayed there more than a week. Special Polish/Canadian units came in next to patrol."

Waking up in the mornings must have felt strange. It took time for the men to accept that there would not be sounds of gunfire. Gone was the fear of being bombed. Vanished was the terror of being blown up as the tanks traveled along the road. Two-thirds of Wilhemshaven had been destroyed by the Allied bombs or from the fighting within. Gray rubble was everywhere. Yet, small patches of green stood out amongst the tree stumps in the parks. The residents were rarely seen in the streets. Those who were seen looked the other way when Allied soldiers came onto their path. Kaz and his men tried to talk to some of them in German. But, only a few children responded if approached. They looked emaciated. They were fearful at first. But, once they received a loaf of bread or a package of cookies, they smiled and a friendly glow filled their eyes. Soon, they ran back to their houses to share their treasures.

It had been a long six years for everyone. The civilian population in many places like Wilhelmshaven had suffered much – from bombs, the fear of being bombed, the anguish for loved ones on the battlefield, or grief for the ones already lost. The most important naval base for the Germans on their own territory, the city had been bombed often. At the end of the fighting, it had become an intense battleground. Most of its buildings had been destroyed. You can imagine how many civilians, including children, had been killed or wounded.

How much more suffering could such families bear? Of course, the enemies had been made to seem like monsters by the Nazy propaganda machine. No wonder the fearful inhabitants now closed themselves in their houses, perhaps huddled together in feelings of hopelessness, not being able to explain to their children why these horrors had been happening.

Fortunately, much of the countryside had been spared. Now, instead of searching with their eyes for possible snipers as the tanks advanced toward their next destination, the men viewed a pastoral scene of cows or sheep grazing the green fields, farmhouses peaceful and well looked after, and occasionally, a farmer plowing his land. The small villages the caravan of tanks passed by were untouched by bombings.

Kaz's troop was ordered to stay temporarily in one of them. The village was located a few kilometers from Osnabruck, the third largest city in Lower Saxony, Germany.

Slowly eased off from the military action, the men were given daily programs. The tanks and equipment were to be cleaned and refitted. The exercise programs and marches were to be attended. Concerts and shows by well-known artists were offered. Men were given lectures on how to relate to the area civilians and what opportunities might be available for the servicemen in the future.

There was also more free time. The village population was friendly. The people were also hungry because the shops had few goods to sell. The canteen for the military was the only place to buy cookies. Kaz gave these to the children he met while strolling in the beautiful and peaceful surroundings.

Some early mornings, he wandered into the forest, to a secluded clearing where he sat alone. He watched the morning dew form on green leaves and he saw multi-colored flowers dry in the sun. He saw how everything in nature sparkled. In humility, he offered his thanks to the Almighty One for the ending of the long ordeal. He asked for help for the previously misguided humanity, for his family with whom he had not communicated for so many years, for his comrades in action, and for himself. He especially asked guidance for a new, meaningful direction.

The city of Osnabruck, a commercial centre and a university town, was the troop's next area of residence. Osnabruck had been an important hub in the early stages of the rising Nazi party. Following its seizure of power in January 1933, the city saw the implementation of the party's economic, political, and social programs. These resulted in a better life for ethnic Germans who did not oppose the new regime. The town went from over 10,000 unemployed in early 1933 to an actual labor shortage by 1938. However, those who did not conform to the established order did not share in this growth. Instead, they found themselves discriminated against, imprisoned, or forced to close their businesses and leave town as Nazi pressure increased. During the war, both Jews and Romany were deported to concentration and extermination camps.

When the war ended, the leading Nazis fled the city. The British, who were now in charge, appointed a new mayor and the British took over more than seventy homes for their own use. Power rested chiefly with the occupiers. Relations between them and the people of

Osnabrück were generally peaceful. But, amidst shortages, the black market thrived and became a main focus of police activity. Tensions existed. Small fights broke out between Allied soldiers and the city's young people. Some Osnabrückers resented the relationships that developed between the occupiers and the local women.

The house where Kaz stayed along with a dozen other soldiers was frequented by women who willingly fraternized and slept with the men in exchange for necessities such as flour, potatoes, and cans of meat. The young women came from as far away as Berlin. And the soldiers, having been deprived of female company for so many years, were more than eager. The troops received cases of wine as an appreciation from French wine makers. Kaz kept most of the wine he received in the closet of his room. When the others who occupied the house ran out of their own supply, they bought some from Kaz. He said, "It was a nice little income! But the situation was not very pleasant for me. You can't imagine what took place in the other rooms of the house!"

Teaching English, Leaving for Canada

Kaz soon discovered that many Polish and Hungarian refugees and former prisoners of war lived in that section of Germany. Among them were students, school teachers, and principals. A Polish principal approached the corps with the idea of organizing a school for young people of Polish heritage. Permission was received. Since a large school nearby was available, it became the venue for teaching high school subjects with emphasis on commerce and English. Instruction was in Polish.

The organizers were looking for help. Once the teachers were hired, they were responsible to the English authority that regulated the curriculum with learning to speak English as one of the required subjects. The challenge was to find a Polish teacher who spoke both languages. Since Kaz's command of English was pretty good, thanks to the help of friends he had met during the war, the principal approached Kaz and said, "You have been selected for a special job."

"What kind of a job?" Kaz asked. He did not know about the school.

"You'll be teaching English in our new Polish school. You will not be there long - perhaps a month," the principal continued. "We hope to find a professional teacher in the meantime." Kaz went to the school in Osnabruck, introduced himself to the faculty, and received a warm welcome. Kaz enjoyed this new challenge of teaching English. He used the guidelines of a teacher's manual, but also introduced discussions in English whenever he could. Most of the students liked the classes. They did their homework, and practiced the language amongst themselves. Two weeks after the starting date, the principal told Kaz that an inspector would come to his class. However, when the inspector came Kaz was so engrossed in teaching that he did not notice him.

Later, when the director congratulated him, Kaz asked, "Congratulations for what?"

"The inspector approved your teaching. There is no need for us to look for anyone else."

Teaching came easy to Kaz because he enjoyed talking with people and he was able to inspire them. The other teachers were kind. They helped mark his papers and arranged parties frequently, which he enjoyed.

Kaz was with the school until 1947 when the Russians complained to the United Nations that the British government was keeping foreign troops in Germany. The British government had to pull the corps out. The time had come when those wanting to return to Poland could go back. Many did go back. Kaz could not return since Poland was under the Communist rule. He knew that, if he went back, he would be either shot or jailed by the authorities.

Kaz chose to go to England. His prospects of getting a job weren't too good. The country had its own returning soldiers, also looking for work. Poles without specific skills would not have chances of being hired.

Kaz and his comrades were housed in an old castle. Kaz said, "It was an interesting place, but really, we were just waiting for a better day. We were well looked after, were well fed. Yet, we did not know what would happen and where we would end up. Eventually, there was a communiqué from our command that emigration to Canada, Australia or New Zealand was now possible. We were to commit ourselves to work in agriculture for two years before seeking other employment. I had some experience in farming, having worked with my father on the family farm. A Polish friend had a degree in agriculture. He said, 'Why don't you apply?' He encouraged me and offered to coach me if needed."

Kaz's choice was Canada. He had read about Canada's vast forests and lakes years ago when he was a forest ranger in Poland and was excited about moving there. He had often thought that, one day, he'd like to visit the country, perhaps even live there. Now that he was to travel across the ocean he remembered the fortune teller's prediction, which he had scoffed at when it had been given.

The government officials did not ask any specific questions and the men were on their way, paid by the army. They were loaded on Aquitania, an old passenger boat. That was June 24 or 25, in 1947. "We arrived in Halifax on the last day of June in the evening. We had to stay on the boat overnight. We disembarked on July 1, which is Dominion Day in Canada. This marked the beginning of my new life in the New World. That is why July 1 is a very memorable day for me."

As an Immigrant

Soldiers in khaki uniforms, many wearing badges of honour, were cheered as they disembarked in Halifax harbour. Wives, children, parents, and siblings of returning Canadian soldiers were present to welcome their loved ones. Kaz watched as people expressed their happiness. Some had brought flowers. A woman wiped away tears of joy while a small boy, standing behind her, hung on to her skirt. The boy did not recognize his father after so many years of absence.

Kaz and his comrades were escorted to a hall where members of a women's service organization gave them a generous welcome. There was much laughter, even some flirting, as the men were served tea, sandwiches, cookies, coffee, and juices. Kaz recalled, "It was unforgettable. But, we did not really have enough time to enjoy the company of these pretty ladies because we had to get on the train. We left Halifax on a special transcontinental train for soldiers, all paid for by the Canadian government. I don't remember how many days we traveled. But, I saw endless stretches of forest where no one had ever stepped. Finally, I ended up in

Toronto with my knapsack and a heavy suitcase full of books."

After an overnight stay in a boarding house, the men were driven to the unemployment office in Newmarket, then a very small village. The prospective farm hands were lined up in a single file. The farmers came in and sized them up. This reminded Kaz of slave trade. The first one to be picked was Kaz's friend, Jon Matenko, a graduate of an agricultural college. He went to work for McNear, a very good farmer.

Kaz was pulled out second by a fellow named Brown, who could not get his car going on leaving the office. During the war, this farmer had struggled to make a living by delivering coal. His wife had been brought up on a farm in Holland. Because of the food shortage, even in Canada, she had encouraged her husband to go into farming. They rented the farm next to McNear. The couple kept dairy cows and egg-producing chickens to feed the family. They had bought old, dilapidated equipment. There was a plow, a cultivator to loosen the ground, and a harrow, which they did not use during the time Kaz was on the farm. Mr. Brown knew little about farming. Therefore, everything seemed to be done by trial and error.

However, Kaz liked the team of the western saddle horses, Bell and Mel, which had been bought to work on the farm. They were not trained for that kind of exertion so the farmer had a lot of trouble in harnessing them for work, as well as getting them back to the barn when they had been grazing on the field. When he finally was able to bring the horses to the barn he beat them with a fork.

While watching this bad treatment, Kaz remembered his cousin in Poland who had served in the cavalry and had to deal with a horse that was difficult to handle. He made it behave in a docile way by giving it sugar cubes. Kaz decided to try this trick. During his free time he walked to a store and bought sugar cubes to give, a few at a time, to Mel and Bell. After a week, the horses came running whenever Kaz called them.

Kaz slept in a room above the chicken coop and the rooster woke him each morning. The farm had no indoor facilities. Therefore, he had to go outside to brush his teeth. On the first day, he was standing outside holding a mug of water in his hand. The family's six-year-old son watched him, then asked, "What are you doing?"

"Don't you see what I am doing?" Kaz asked him.

"You have a brush in your mouth," the boy remarked, puzzled.

"I am brushing my teeth. Don't you do that?"

"No," answered the little boy.

It was July. The haying season had just started. The farmer had no mechanical equipment for cutting or stacking the hay. It had to be pitched with a fork. The weather was hot and the work was strenuous. After the first week, Kaz's hands were numb. He asked to go to a doctor and Mr. Brown took him to one. Upon examining him, the doctor asked about his background. Kaz explained that he was a former soldier and had been teaching school since the end of the war in northern Germany. The doctor's opinion was that, since Kaz was not used to such strenuous work, he might get a paralysis if he does not ease off. However, he managed to work through the haying season. There were no other crops to harvest.

In addition to the son, the family had two daughters. They were perhaps ten and twelve years old. The mother had assigned special jobs to them. They set the table for meals and cleaned up afterwards. The girls had blisters around their finger nails and Kaz thought that they might have some infection. When they set the table and handled the food with these fingers, Kaz found it so unappetizing that he no longer wanted to eat with the family. On his day off, he walked to a store and bought himself Polish sausage and bread. He ate that instead of joining the family at mealtimes.

After two or three days the farmer asked, "Why are you not eating?"

"I don't feel like it," Kaz answered.

"But you cannot work if you do not eat," insisted the concerned farmer.

"Don't I do my work?" asked Kaz.

The farmer had to agree that Kaz did do his work, "Yes, but how long will you be able to keep on like this?"

"I don't know," Kaz answered honestly.

"I notice that you are not very happy here," the farmer noted.

Kaz did not disagree, "I like your horses, but that is actually all," he said.

"You know what your privileges are? You can go to the employment office and tell them you want to change your place of work." Mr. Brown was fair on that score.

Kaz let the employment office in Newmarket know that he was unhappy with his situation. The office manager looked at his papers and told him that he did not actually belong to that office.

"How did I end up here?" Kaz asked.

"A good question!" was the answer.

When Kaz arrived at the Toronto office, the manager was away. But Kaz spoke about his work experience with the office workers on duty. They did not believe his story. However, the following day an inspector went to check out the farm where Kaz had been working. He did not even enter the buildings. By merely looking around, he could see that the farm was run down and was not suitable for a placement.

"We're going to take you out of there," the inspector said.

"What are you going to do with me?" asked Kaz.

"I don't know. We'll see." He told Kaz to report to the employment office once a day.

A few days later, a commissioner spoke to Kaz, "We have a place for you, but it's in northern Ontario.

"Oh, Timmins!"

"How do you know?"

"Oh, I know a little geography," Kaz answered.

"You are going to work on a chicken farm. As soon as we have the contract ready, we're going to ship you over." He added, "My son, Bill Wallace, works in Timmins as a food chain store manager. Get in touch with him!" He gave Kaz Bill's phone number and address.

On his arrival in Timmins, Kaz discovered that the chicken farm was located outside the city. The farmer had a four-story chicken coop. But, he had run out of money to mechanize it. His workers had to carry water and food by hand. Sometimes, they worked until two in the morning sorting eggs.

"We had no days off," recalled Kaz. "But the food was good. The plates were clean and I was allowed to live within the farmhouse instead of in the chicken coop." Kaz told me. "Finally, I persuaded the farmer to give me a day off and asked to use his phone. I called Bill Wallace and he invited me to his house. I think the farmer was surprised that I knew anyone in the area.

"At Bill Wallace's home," Kaz recalled, "we played bridge. Two of his friends were also visiting. The man across the table from me was the manager of the local employment agency. Learning about my place of work he divulged that the farmer had been charged with smuggling drugs and bootlegging. Then, he asked how the farmer treated his farm hands. I told him about the long hours we had to work."

"He does not know about the labour laws," said Bill Wallace, looking at his friend. "You better go and tell him."

"I will send someone to talk to him," promised Bill's friend.

The manager of the employment agency sent one of his staff the next day. The young man talked to the farmer. Then he told Kaz, "I told him about the law. If he is not going to abide by it we are going to take you away from his farm."

The farmer became arrogant. Kaz reported him to the office.

"Fine, we are going to pull you out," said the manager.

Kaz had started work on the chicken farm in the beginning of November. It was now around Christmas. He left the farm and was provided lodging in Timmins, where he had to report to the employment office every day. Within a month, a suitable placement was found for him in a large timber company. "You are going to look after horses," the employment manager said.

"Great," Kaz enthused. "I like horses."

The company had a lumber camp with twenty-four horses to pull the logs. It also had: a sawmill, a planing mill, and a carpentry shop. There was even a car dealership just outside of Timmins. On arrival, Kaz was introduced to Alex, the superintendent.

On his farm assignments, Kaz had earned $45 a month (plus room and board), whereas a Canadian farm hand earned $150 a month. Kaz's salary was less than one-third of what any other worker received. And, the government contract stipulated that the veteran was to work under the signed contract at least for two years. Why had the Canadian Government agreed to such an unsound deal for men who had risked their lives for freedom?

The timber company paid Kaz eighty-five cents an hour. But Kaz had to pay his own room and board. He roomed with a French Canadian lady. She was talkative and told him stories about the parishioners of the Catholic Church. For instance, if a young couple got married and did not have a child within a certain time period, the priest would go to their home to find out what was wrong. In one case, the husband was an alcoholic. This caused tension and arguments, especially about money he was to bring home weekly. The wife finally arranged for the company to deposit his paycheck directly into their bank account. She said that she prayed for her husband and a miracle occurred. He stopped drinking and became a normal man. They then had children and were happy.

Working with the horses was an easy job. Much of the time, Kaz had nothing to do. He finally went to the carpenter's shop to speak with Ray, the manager. Kaz liked the fellow and thought that he might enjoy working with him.

"Could I be of some help?" Kaz asked.

"Sure," Ray said.

So Kaz started to work in the shop. One day, the superintendent came in. On seeing Kaz working he said, "What are you doing here? You're supposed to be in the barn."

Ray answered, "We can use him here. The work in the barn leaves him a lot of free time."

Alex said, "I don't mind, as long as the horses are looked after."

Kaz learned to make storm doors with screens and glasses. At some point, one of the workers became ill. Ray asked Kaz, "Do you think that you have learned enough to work by yourself? An urgent order for twelve doors has just come in."

"With your help, I can try." Kaz answered. Roy helped him and it took them twice as long, but they succeeded. This made Kaz happy.

Later, while recalling his early life in Poland, Kaz remembered that his Aunt Stephania's husband had written about the Americans and how they prepare themselves for retirement. "A part of the money you make as a young man is put aside to give you security for old age. Life insurance is a good way to save," he had written.

Kaz investigated and received four or five proposals from different insurance companies. He also learned that there was a difference among insurance policies. "Feeling really confused, I went to Bill and asked him to help me," Kaz remembered.

"I don't know much more than you do, but perhaps our accountant can help," Bill answered.

Together, they sorted out the different options and decided that Mutual Life of Canada had the best offer. Kaz applied for an insurance policy which cost him $39.15 every three months. This included a retirement program which would give him security once he reached sixty-five. While preparing the documents, the branch manager was so impressed with Kaz's knowledge that he asked him to become an agent.

Kaz was really surprised, "What are you talking about?" he asked. "I wouldn't know what to do."

"Never mind, we'll train you," the manager assured him.

Kaz responded, "I have a six month left of my contract with the government."

"I will ask the company to write a letter to the Minister of Labour to have you released."

Unfortunately, the Minister of Labour did not want to release him. The manager was told that, if Kaz was that good, the company could wait for him. However, he was allowed to work in the insurance business part time until the two-year contract was fulfilled.

Kaz recalled, "So, the insurance company provided me with a little bit of training. Then, they licensed me. At that time, I was teaching English to some displaced people in my spare time. Realizing that half of the students did not have insurance, I sold insurance policies to many of them. The people in the office could not get over how many applications I brought in.

"Eventually, I ran out of customers. I had to go out to seek for them. I was taking classes. I can't remember what I was learning. There, I met a classmate who was a hydro engineer working in a mine, which had a strike at that time. When this classmate found out that I was in the insurance business, he suggested that I should go to that mine and give a presentation.

"I wrote to the insurance company and asked for some presentation material. It was all on a film. There were no videos or CDs at that time. I got two films and encouraged other agents to go. But, they were not interested. They thought it was too far, so I went by myself on a week-end. I received a great welcome. The superintendent had everything ready, including the projector. I showed the film, and then asked those who were interested to come to the office which had been set up for the occasion. There was a line-up of people and I was writing applications until two in the morning! I insured every family except one. Twenty-four applications!"

"Wow! How did you do that?" the other agents asked with envy when Kaz returned.

He tried similar ventures later but with less success.

Planning Life together with Doris

The annual Sadie Hawkins dance was a popular affair in Timmins in the late forties. Bernice, who worked in the same insurance company office, invited Kaz to go with her.

"I'm not much of a dancer," Kaz admitted. However, persuaded by the young woman, Kaz did go.

During the evening, he stood on the side lines watching the dancers. Bernice came to introduce Kaz to her former teacher, Doris Fenner. Kaz recalled, "She was attractive and we had a lively conversation. I don't remember what we talked about, but it was something both of us enjoyed. She was very straightforward and real. This started our relationship. We met in her apartment often. Little by little, we got to know each other.

"We exchanged our thoughts about life. We teased each other and at times we had lively, yet not too serious disputes. Often, we talked about our purpose in life, asking how we could live that purpose. On that score, we complemented each other.

"Doris wanted to have a family and was very eager to get married. To me, it didn't really matter."

To Kaz, their relationship was nothing like 'falling in love.' They both believed what someone wise had said, "Love is not about finding the right person, but creating a right relationship. It's not about how much love you have in the beginning, but how much love you build till the end."

On Valentine's Day in 1950, they sat in Doris' living room listening to the broadcast of the election speech Winston Churchill had given that day in Edinburgh. He concluded the speech with:

"What prizes lie before us;
Peace, food, happiness, leisure,
Wealth for the masses never known or dreamed of;
The glorious advance into period of rest and safety
For all the hundreds of millions of homes,
Where little children play by the fire,
And girls grow up in all their beauty,
And young men march to fruitful labour in all their strength and valour.
Let us not shut out the hope, that the burden of fear and want
May be lifted for a glorious era from the bruised and weary shoulders of mankind."

Inspired by the speech, they sat in silence for a long time, thinking what it meant for their possible life together. It was that evening when they came to believe they could make go of it. So, Kaz and Doris decided they would marry. They were happy. Right from the beginning Doris had called Kaz her Polish Prince and she appealed to him in many ways.

The wedding was planned for June that year. Since Doris was not Catholic, the ceremony took place in an Anglican church in Toronto. Kaz's friend from the army, Jon Matenko, was the best man and one of Doris' friends was the bridesmaid. The reception was held at her friend's place since Doris' parents had already moved from their large house to an apartment. Because of strong insurance sales, Kaz had won a free holiday at the prestigious Signor y Club in Montebello. That was where the couple spent their honeymoon.

Soon afterwards, while they were still living in Timmins, Kaz's good friend was transferred to a branch manager's position in Sudbury. He wanted Kaz to come with him. Kaz agreed. Needing more clients for his insurance business, he thought that, since Sudbury would be a brand new territory, his business would improve. Doris also asked for a transfer from her school board and was hired as a physical education teacher in Sudbury.

Finding a rental accommodation in that city was a challenge. "You have to buy," a real estate agent suggested. Doris phoned her father who had promised to help if needed and, indeed, he helped the newlyweds. They found a house owned by a Canadian and his English war bride who was homesick and wanted to go back to England. Priced for a quick sale, the house was cheaper than it would have been otherwise. The furniture was for sale, as well. "So, we got the whole shebang, including some dishes," recalled Kaz.

The couple who owned the house wanted to leave for England the following month. Doris and Kaz went back to Timmins to liquidate their belongings, Kaz from the house owned by a nice family, and Doris from her apartment. Before they moved, they had not realized that the new home was close to a railway track. The first night, when the train went by, the house shook. Kaz jumped out of bed thinking that it was an earthquake. But after a week, both of them were so used to the noise they hardly heard it.

Doris started teaching and Kaz looked for prospects to sell insurance. He had a terrible time. Sudbury had many French Canadian people who were not inclined to buy insurance. After many rejections, Kaz decided to quit. But what was he going to do? He had no idea.

Sudbury was grey from smoke at that time, and smelly from sulfur in the air. Everything for five kilometres around it was bare, burned out. The farmers in the area had trouble growing crops. They filed claims and the large mining company, Inco, paid the cost of the losses. However, the Canadian government demanded that the matter be properly investigated. A scientist who did this research lived on the first floor of the Chomko house. His conclusion was that a high chimney had to be built.

Inco built the high chimney. It also began to build a town for the miners. "Perhaps, I should try my hand at carpentry!" Kaz decided. "And, one day, I got the nerve to go over to the manager of the site to ask for a job. I told him a few lies about my experience."

"We subcontract," the manager said. "We need someone to hang the doors inside and outside." Kaz was told.

Kaz had never hung a door in his life. He went to the library to study the right procedure and in a short time he learned a lot of theory which he began to put into practice. "The manager offered me so much per door, perhaps $10.00. I was making a very small wage out of that because I did not have practical experience. But I learned short cuts. In the traditional way, a frame is built for the door and the carpenter fits the door to the frame. But that was a tedious way of doing it. I learned that you can measure the door, and then make the frame to suit the door, not the other way around. Over a period of two weeks, I doubled my production."

"You are making too much money. We are going to cut your pay," the manager told Kaz. They did and Kaz was still making good money at $5 per door. That must have been in 1952.

Building a Home and Friendships

Doris and Kaz began to think about another move, perhaps closer to Toronto. She suggested, "Why don't you go and stay with my brother and scout for a place?" Her brother, Bruce, was away most of the time because he was surveying the Trans-Canada Highway.

Kaz went to Toronto. By visiting a different real estate office each day, he learned that houses around Toronto were extremely expensive. One day, he went to Ajax. Someone suggested that he talk to an agent from a real estate firm which owned a holiday resort with cottages to rent.

The agent said, "You can buy some of these cottages. Or, how about building something for yourself?" He had a five-acre piece of open land and offered it at a good price. Kaz liked the idea of building a home on an open field, having been raised in a rural area. However, he did not make a commitment. He went home to discuss it with Doris. She came down and liked it.

The plan was for Kaz to rent a place to stay, find a job, and then, eventually, to start building the house. He found a big house owned by a lady, who provided him with room and board. And while working for a construction company in Scarborough during the day, he spent his evenings planning the house.

Doris was a veteran and so was Kaz. Therefore, they were eligible for the Veterans Land Act. They chose a beautiful plan for a bungalow and presented it to the representative of the VLA. He considered it too expensive. They presented another, a split level plan with no bathroom upstairs. VLA accepted that plan.

Kaz hired a contractor to dig the basement and a well digger to dig the well. Dowsing with a branch, the man found a source of water ten feet from the house. "That is the best source, lots of good water," he said.

Debating whether to lay the foundation himself or contract it out, Kaz finally decided to save money and lay his own basement. He made a lot of mistakes, but the VLA inspector approved it. Kaz was surprised and happy, having never done a foundation before. Then followed the building of the joists, the floor, the walls and the roof.

All this work was done in his spare time. Kaz often worked until eleven in the evening when the lights went out in the district. If anything had happened, no one would have known. "Working on the roof at night was beautiful," Kaz recalled. "The stars and the moon seemed closer even only at ten feet from the ground," he remembered. Kaz had started the work on the house in the fall of 1952. The family moved in the following year.

Doris was pregnant. She was alone at home when her labour pains started. The taxi she took to the hospital slipped into a ditch because of the icy road, but luckily she arrived at the hospital on time. Kaz was working when he received the call. He rushed to the hospital when told about the delivery. Of course he was very happy to know that Doris and his new son were both well! Doris' maternity leave from the school lasted for two months. When Doris went to work, her mother looked after the baby.

In the spring of 1954, Kaz was still painting the walls of the house. One day, when Doris had gone somewhere, Kaz found three-year-old Richard sitting in the middle of a puddle painting himself. "You are painting the house and I am painting myself," he seemed to say. Running after the cat around the house was one of Richard's favourite games. The cat had become part of the family when Kaz was preparing their move from Sudbury. The emaciated mouser had crawled into Kaz's panel truck. The first time he threw her out. She kept returning obviously wanting to move. So, the grey and black striped cat became a family member. When they were settled in the new house, the cat used to come to Kaz's side and meow whenever she wanted to go out.

For Christmas, in 1953, the Chomko family invited their good friend, Ted Tass, and his family for a visit. Doris cooked a turkey in a small range because the kitchen did not have a stove yet. Kaz recalled, "It was amazing, the way this girl prepared it. It was delicious!"

The following year, Ted and his family wanted to move closer. Kaz explored the area for a good jeweler. He found one for Ted to work with. Good friends since their meeting in Holland during the winning part of the war, Ted and Kaz had been in the same regiment. Kaz explained, "Each regiment had a repair unit. Anyone within the regiment could call for help. Some repairmen were trained for mechanical things. Some were trained for electrical. Gunmen were trained to look after the guns. Ted was in the gunner crew.

"While in Mark Canal in Holland, my platoon was dispatched close to the sea coast in order to stop the Jerries from withdrawal. We got ourselves into a hot spot. Each day, a different tank took the lead. On that particular day, my tank was in the front. I got hit by the Jerries' 88mm gun from two miles away. As a result, my gun was immobilized. I radioed to my squadron commander for help. There was only a terrible silence!

They knew that I was in a very difficult situation because of a mine field around us. Ted received the message. On his own, he came through the minefield to help me. He found me there, helpless. We threw a smoke grenade to hide us as we backed out. It was a very dangerous day!"

That was Kaz's first meeting with Ted on a personal basis. Ted was around thirty years old then. He had joined the Polish army as a teenager in order to become a professional soldier. During the war, he had become part of the regular army personnel and served in a repair unit. Because Ted had endangered himself when Kaz in trouble, they became friends. They continued to have close contact with each other throughout their lives.

When the war was over, Kaz's troop liberated a camp of women prisoners who had been imprisoned for being involved in a rebellion in Warsaw against the Nazis. The soldiers received a royal welcome and made friends with many of them. Ted had not been part of the liberation force since the repair units were always behind, but Kaz wanted Ted to meet some of the girls. Away they went and met a group of girls who had known each other in civilian life. Amongst these girls Ted found his special one. He and Barbara fell in love in a most romantic way and they were married soon afterwards.

As for Kaz, he had flirted with several of the young women, but he did not want a relationship. The only commitment he wanted, at that time, was his job as the tank commander. He wanted to do that job well.

Ted and Barbara ended up in England after the war, but Kaz and Ted wrote regularly. In one of his letters, Ted told about the shortage of consumable goods in England. Everything was still rationed and people were hungry. Kaz and Doris, who lived in Sudbury at the time, invited the couple and their daughter, Sophia, to come to Canada. Ted and Barbara applied for immigration and were accepted. Kaz rented a place for them and picked them up at the Toronto airport.

Ted began to work at the mines and made good money. But, a mine is a dangerous and dirty place to work and Ted was not that strong. While in England, he had received training in jewelry making. He had made silver rings with the Scottish thistle as a motif and initials with a flower on the other side.

While working in the mine, Ted searched and he found a jeweler who hired him to do watch work. He worked in the jewelry store for nine years, and then was laid off. (If someone worked for a private enterprise for more than ten years, the employer would have to start contributing to the employee's pension.) Now, Ted's future work was in jeopardy. He came to ask his friend for advice and Kaz said, "There is a good jeweler in

Oshawa. Perhaps you should see him about a job." Ted went to the store, had an interview, and was hired. He worked there for a long time while dreaming about starting his own business.

Kaz had sold an insurance policy to Ted and Barbara soon after they immigrated to Canada. They borrowed from the policy, moved to Oshawa, and built a house. Ted took a training course in Toronto in diamond cutting and, when he had saved enough, he started his own business.

One day, in 1955, an insurance man from Oshawa called Kaz. The agent had come across a policyholder in Timmins who had told him, "Kaz Chomko would be an excellent salesman for your company."

"How would you like to come back into the insurance business?" the agent asked Kaz. "It may be a long process before you can make a living, but we'll put you on a monthly salary until you are on your feet."

The bank manager loaned Kaz enough money to buy a new car, based on Doris' salary. Kaz sold his old 'bump bump', as Richard called the old car. So Kaz was back in the insurance business. The few Polish people he knew were hard to convince to buy insurance. So were the others he approached. He struggled with the business for almost three years. Finally, he told the agent, "Pat, I can't make a go of it!"

"Stay a little longer!" Pat pleaded. Kaz did but the business did not improve.

Back to the carpentry! At this time Kaz worked for the Dunlop Tire Company in Whitby. Kaz had to join the union if he wanted the job. He paid for the initiation and a regular monthly fee and he worked for the company as a carpenter for over a year.

In the meantime, Doris was at home with Richard and Robert, who was born in 1954. Soon afterwards, Doris was approached by a principal from an Ajax High School who knew her from their teacher's training period. He offered her a job in his school.

"What about the children?" Kaz asked. Doris decided to look for a caregiver. She finally she found a lady who lived in the northern part of Ajax. She agreed to take care of the children in her home while Doris was teaching. Richard, then three, did not like the arrangement. While in the backyard of the lady's house, he got the notion to go to his mother. The school where she worked was in the southern part of Ajax. Traffic was congested on the bridge as Richard headed toward the school. His caregiver discovered that he was missing and gave his description to the police who, luckily, found Richard unharmed. When Kaz arrived to pick him up, he dashed to his father's arms, tears flowing down his face.

When Doris' mother, whom the children called Nanny, came to live with the family, Richard was already in school. But, after school, Nanny used to take them to the lake shore, where they made sand castles and threw rocks into the water. As the time went on, Nanny could not walk all the way to the shore anymore. So she would sit down on a log to watch them from a distance.

Nanny bought the family a television. It was placed in the dining room which had become Nanny's bedroom. On weekend mornings, the boys loved to sit with her and watch the pheasants and rabbits as they jumped into the fenced-in chicken pen for food. The boys had fun with Nanny every day. A checker board under his arm, Robert used to climb up on her bed to play checkers with her. She always let him win.

Robert had a great interest in learning. He would listen to the adults while they were talking and would stop them to ask them what a word meant. His parents wanted to get him into some form of preschool. A public school near Ajax offered nothing for very young children. Still an Anglican, Doris went to check out a Catholic school run by Franciscan sisters. She liked what she saw and Robert was accepted in the preschoolers' class. Doris used to take him there in the morning on her way to school. The sisters kindly kept him there until she was able to pick him up.

This was a turning point in Doris' religion. Kaz was a member of the Knights of Columbus and received their magazine, *Columbia*. The back page had an article about people wanting to become Catholic. One day, Doris said to Kaz, "I am interested in becoming a Catholic! I am going to write to them." She received a letter suggesting she find a local priest to give her guidance. Kaz approached a priest in Ajax and Doris began to prepare herself.

They had been married in an Anglican church. Kaz recalled, "When Doris became a Catholic, we went through the whole shebang. We were privately remarried and the children were re-baptized. I found out later that an Anglican baptism is valid in the Catholic Church. As time went on, Doris found out how much richer our church is compared to the Anglican. Catholic is the true apostolic church!"

In the meantime, the family had developed an extensive garden on their farm. Kaz subscribed to a fruit growers' magazine in which he saw an advertisement for special raspberry canes – a cross between purple and red. He ordered some from a supplier in Niagara Falls and planted them as an experiment. The results were excellent. Eventually, he had a whole acre of raspberry bushes.

One day, when an inspector from the Veterans Land Act Department came to visit, he indicated that the department could help out, "We can consolidate all your debts and can re-classify you as a small holding. You have to do a little work, though." He gave Kaz a book of forms to be filled out with figures. When filled out and approved, the farm could be re-classified.

Unsure about the year, Kaz speculated, "It must have been around 1960, because Robert was in school already. The boys went to a Catholic school where the smart ones had to follow a different curriculum and both of them had high grades. But the sister used to give them too much homework. Why do you pile so much work on them? I asked."

"They can handle it!" the sister told Kaz.

"If you don't ease up," Kaz told her, "I am going to take them out. Do they have to be on an honour roll? No, they don't as long as they have good marks."

The production on the farm improved consistently for a couple years. Kaz had hired foreign workers to pick up the berries and the farm was doing well. But then Chrysler Corporation opened a parts manufacturing plant in Ajax and hired anyone who wanted to work. They paid higher salaries than Kaz could afford. Because of this factory, the Chomko farm lost most of its workers. The business was in trouble and Kaz did not know what to do. Finally, having learned from an American fruit growers' magazine about 'Pick Your Own', he advertised. But he could not get enough people to pick the crop. Therefore, the production had to be reduced. That, of course, reduced the income. In desperation, Kaz phoned the Department of Agriculture and asked for advice.

The representatives came and said that, with five acres of land, he could go into hog production. Kaz investigated and found out that hog production farms were called mortgage lifters. But he did not know anything about hogs. So, he visited a few farms to learn something about hog production.

On one of these tours, Kaz met a man working for a research laboratory. His name was Dr. Crawley and he overheard the conversation Kaz had with a farmer. "How would you like to join us?" Dr. Crawley asked. "We are trying to breed a new kind of a hog. The piglets are delivered by cesarean section."

"Why is that necessary?" asked Kaz, puzzled.

"If they are born the natural way they get infected with pneumonia and rhinitis," Dr. Crawley explained.

Kaz was interested but the buildings on his farm were not adequate. There was only the house, an equipment shed, and a small chicken pen. So, again, Kaz went to the Department of Agriculture for help with the new buildings. The government even provided him with the plan for what to do and how to build a new barn.

Dr. Crawley suggested that it should have slatted floors. This would eliminate the cleaning problem. The main barn, which would be used to raise the pigs for meat, would have a slatted floor and the basement would be waterproof. The plan was followed. Everything was automated.

The research lab supplied the male piglets. They were raised to market size, and then sold. But the facilities were not suitable for mother sows. One day Dr. Crawley said, "Why don't you build another barn?"

They did. Kaz called it "the maternity ward." It had room for twenty sows which were already pregnant when brought to the farm. They had to be in special crates so that they could not turn around because some of them could eat their piglets when they were born. This particular establishment was like a hospital. Hygiene was most important. Only three people were allowed in. They were Kaz, the veterinarian, and a representative from the lab. In order to enter into the maternity ward, they had to wear special clothes, have a foot bath, disinfect, and wear surgical gloves.

Health Challenges

The project was doing well until chronic arthritis struck Kaz in 1967. It became such a problem that he was unable to work. The business could not be sold as a going enterprise because the directors of the research lab did not want anyone running it unless they were knowledgeable about the venture. Therefore, it had to be dismantled. The lab bought most of the pigs. The rest were sold on an open market. Soon afterwards, Kaz and Doris sold the house, the barn, and the five acres of land.

Kaz recalled, "We moved to Oshawa where Ted and his family were living. Doris was offered a teaching job with the Durham Catholic School Board and the boys moved to McClaughlin High School to continue their education. Richard had a bit of trouble in high school. He used to think a lot and the teacher accused him of daydreaming. Also, he had a stammer early on. We took him to many specialists for speech improvement. His speech did improve, little by little.

"My left hip gave me more and more trouble. It was very painful. Finally, I had a surgery in Toronto. I had suffered the original injury during wartime. But, I don't remember when it had happened. The tank parts are all metal and often we were so tired that we slept sitting up inside! When we had to refuel, it was usually after midnight by the time we were finished. I would then climb on the turret and fall asleep. I was so tired."

The cartilage around Kaz's hip joint had calcified. While he was walking, it rubbed against the bone and crumbled to become like sand. Through the years, this problem had developed into painful arthritis. After the operation, Kaz felt a little better. He worked for a small firm selling houses while Doris was teaching.

During the summer of 1969, the family went on a holiday to eastern Canada. When in the Halifax area, Kaz recalled, "We let the boys loose and made arrangements to meet them each day at lunch. They did not always show up. They were too busy—each in his own way. But, they eventually appeared when they got very hungry. After Halifax, we spent a week on Prince Edward Island and ate lobster. It was my first time ever. I liked it. Doris did not. Richard was not sure. But, Robert did like it. Then we drove to Montreal for a couple of days. Since our time was running out, we came home. The traveling experience was good. It gave us a new perspective on our life in Canada. Doris went back to teaching. The boys went back to school, and I went back to my real estate business.

"The following year, we traveled again. This time, we went to the west coast. We had quite an experience coming out of Ontario. We did not realize that the speed limit had changed in Manitoba. We finally got stopped by a Mountie. He said to Robert who was driving, 'You know that you are breaking the law? The speed limit is sixty.' He gave us a ticket which was a good warning!

"After several days, we ended up on Vancouver Island. Doris had friends in Campbellford, in the northern part of the island. She was determined to visit them. But, we had a real job to find them. While driving around and looking for the town, we encountered some hippies planting corn. They did not have a clue how to go about it, but they tried. I gave them a few instructions. Finally, we arrived in the woods where Doris' friends lived and enjoyed three days with these friends who had gone to school with Doris many years ago. Then, we visited Nanaimo and, finally, Victoria, which is such a beautiful place."

A New Phase in Life as a Deacon

Before leaving for the west coast, Kaz had two substantial real estate cases to close. He asked a person whom he considered a good friend to look after them. The friend readily agreed. "On my return," Kaz said, "I found out, to my surprise, that the credit was not given to me but to this false friend. I became discouraged."

Doris noticed his disappointment. "Why don't you quit?" she asked her husband. "You are not supposed to do that kind of work. Something more suitable for you will come up."

"What am I going to do?" asked Kaz, dejectedly.

"Do nothing at least for now. I am making money enough for both of us. We have always been frugal the way we live," Doris pointed out. "We'll manage fine!"

Kaz did not need more coaxing. He filed his application to leave the real estate firm and felt relieved. This was in the fall of 1972.

This change freed Kaz to do charitable work with the Vincent de Paul Society in Toronto, for which he felt he was more suited. The Society's large campground in Penetanguishine had been closed for the winter. Kaz drove with his friend, George Morley, to the camp in order to prepare it for the following summer. On their arrival, they discovered that the camp was in a very bad shape. There were broken storm doors, rickety beds, and broken screens.

Kaz said, "George, this is a big job!"

"Well, we have to fix it up, don't we?" George answered.

In the early 70's the government paid for labour costs for a public service while the charitable organization supplied the materials. When Kaz discussed the project with the local Member of Parliament, he said, "No problem. Make an application and we'll provide the labour costs!"

While preparing for the work, Kaz told George, the chairman of the camp committee, "I saw good bed frames in Toronto."

"What do you like them for?" asked George.

"We could get rid of the rickety ones and make new beds," Kaz explained.

"Oh, that's a good idea," George agreed.

They made a dozen beds for each cabin and bought new mattresses. The work on fixing the screens took from April to June. Kaz and Doris spent the summer helping at the camp. After the program was over, they returned to Oshawa. But, the following year, Doris took a teaching job in Midland, where they lived and worked for three years. Many changes took place at the camp. The dining hall was restored and a large cabin accommodating twelve people was winterized.

The camp chaplain, Msg. Romara, encouraged Kaz to study to become a deacon. He said, "Kaz, I want you to apply for it. When finished, you can help the priests to look after the tourists in the summer and then take a break in the winter time."

Kaz asked, "How could I possibly serve the Lord any better than I am doing now? My wife and I are both involved in the camp. And after it closes, we are free to do what we want. We enjoy what we're doing!"

"Yes, you are doing a wonderful job with this camp," agreed the camp chaplain. "But you are forgetting two important things. By going to the seminary, you are going to gain enlightened understanding of yourself by studying with others. Secondly, the sacrament of ordination will give you the get up and go in a spiritual sense."

Kaz thought about these two points seriously. He was convinced, so he applied.

After closing the camp in 1974, Kaz bought a motor home. He said he wanted to 'gypsy around' and visit Richard, who had moved to Calgary to get away from his parents.

"You're making a big mistake," Doris said. "You're going to be accepted to study in the seminary. What are you going to do then with the motor home?"

Kaz protested, "From a hundred and five applications, only twenty-five will be accepted for the program. My chances are very slim!"

"You answered every question they asked you," Doris reminded him.

Sure enough! A few weeks later, Kaz received a letter from the bishop's office saying that he had been accepted into the program. What was he to do with the motor home?

"I'll ask Richard to sell it!" he decided, and Richard did sell it.

For the next two years, Kaz attended the seminary. He was ordained on June 5, 1976. Since Doris and Kaz lived in Midland, it became Kaz's liturgical base. He became a deacon in St. Margaret Church, the home church for English-speaking Catholics in that area. The pastor, whom everyone called Moose, did not like anyone who wasn't a priest to work with him. But, he liked what Kaz was doing. Kaz registered all the people in the parish who needed help and every weekend Kaz and Doris traveled to St Augustine's seminary in Scarborough to learn more. There, they exchanged methods of work and enjoyed parties for the deacons and their wives.

The term *deacon* comes from a Greek word *diaconos*, meaning servant or minister. In the early church, the first seven deacons were ordained by the Apostles. The first community of Christians were two groups: the Palestinian men and the Greek widows. The main work of the church was to support needy people. The Greek widows complained that they were not being treated equally. That matter ended up with the Apostles who instructed, "Why don't you select, among yourselves, seven men that you can trust. We will give them a little training and then you will work with them."

Kaz's ordination as a deacon took place at St. Michael's Cathedral. The class size had shrunk during the two years of training. One man had died. One man had pulled out because his wife did not like it. A Jamaican man had had a dispute with his bishop and had, therefore, withdrawn.

Since Kaz chose to look after the needs of home-bound people, he had to take additional pastoral training at St Michael's Hospital. For that, he used to travel to downtown Toronto by himself. Doris did not want to go because it was at night.

An Anglican priest and a psychologist were teaching. Kaz remembered the following instruction, "Recognize that you are branded people as deacons. You are going to be watched for your behavior. You must strive for perfection. You have to practice and learn to increase your discipline, for there will be many temptations. You have to test yourself, from time to time, to see if you are strong enough to resist the temptations."

There were many other instructions for self-improvement. They also taught physical exercises along with the spiritual ones. For instance, the newly ordained deacons learned how to relax by lying on the floor while thinking of nothing but the Creator.

After one of these sessions, while driving back to Midland, Kaz thought about this testing himself. "When on the highway I was thinking about self-improvement. At that time, I was a heavy smoker. I could almost hear the voice from the back of the car saying, 'Test yourself!' Oh boy! After the surgery, I had not smoked for six months. Gradually, I began to smoke a pipe. Then I went back to cigarettes.

"This message persisted in my mind; 'Test yourself. Test yourself!' In desperation, I said, 'Lord, I will try— with your help!' That was the deal. North of Barrie, on the road to Midland, I used to light up because I could slow down. I had a pack of cigarettes in my pocket and the old habit persisted. I took a cigarette from the packet. But, the message flashed through my mind. 'Remember, we made a deal!' 'Oh, thank you Lord!' I said. I put the cigarette back into my pocket.

"When I arrived home, everything was quiet. Doris had gone to bed. So I made myself a cup of coffee. That's when I used to light up. The message flashed to me again. 'Remember, we made a deal!' 'Thank you Lord,' I said to myself. I put the cigarette back into my pocket.

"Every time I reached for a cigarette I got this message. Thank you Lord! Finally, every time I had an urge to smoke, I asked for help. The help came. I did not have any problems, no withdrawal symptoms. I did not require any medical help. My friends in Midland noticed, so I told them. One of them tried it, and was successful. But, the others did not even try. They made themselves promises to do it later. However, I knew that, if we do not trust, the promises we make do not stand.

"After the ordination, Doris suggested that we have a little party in our large back yard. We invited Richard to come from Calgary and, of course, Robert came. We bought wine and beer, and borrowed tables from the hall across the street. An Anglican Minister and his wife were our friends. They and many other people came. Robert served the wine. Richard dished out the beer. It was very nice, really."

Kaz and Doris lived in Midland on Easy Street. They stayed in the area until 1981. The boys lived in the family home in Oshawa while the neighbors watched what was going on. One day, a paddy car pulled into the driveway. "Oh, oh! The Chomko boys got into trouble," our neighbors thought. But that was not the case. The police had had an auction sale of unclaimed stolen bikes and Richard and Robert had bought several of them for parts.

Doris had not had any health problems in her life until she noticed that her swallowing became restricted. Her family doctor recommended a throat, nose and ear specialist, who discovered that a cancerous tumor had developed in her throat. This was a serious blow to her, Kaz, and the boys. It took time for her to accept that, at least for the time being, she had to slow down and take care of herself instead of always taking care of others.

A couple of ladies at the Franciscan House urged her, "Go to Father Perna. He will pray for you and you will be healed!" Doris did that, and felt that the lump was decreasing. She had several sessions with Father Perna.

When Kaz and Doris considered moving closer to Toronto, a friend suggested, "If you want to move, how about St. Lawrence parish in Scarborough?"

"That would interest us," Kaz responded. "But we need a place to live."

"I know a widow who has a suitable place for you," the friend encouraged. Kaz and Doris rented the place and Kaz was transferred to St. Lawrence parish. But, Kaz's health also continued to deteriorate. Father Perna prayed for him, as well, and said. "Kaz, the Lord will heal you." But Kaz was a 'doubting Thomas'. By 1986, his arthritis was so bad that he asked to be released from the deacon's duties. However, Bishop Doyle said, "You haven't legs, but you have a good head."

Robert and his wife, Lisa, invited his parents, at least temporarily, to live with them in their farmhouse, where he had created a separate living quarters for them. Robert's daughter Katrina was, at that time, two years old and she liked to come to visit. There would be a little knock, knock, knock. Katrina would be standing at the door asking for 'thoot' (juice). To Kaz, it sounded like truth.

Doris had regular visits to her doctor and after one of the examinations he asked, "What has happened to your growth? It is almost gone." She told him about the priest.

"Oh, I understand!" he said. But, eventually, she had an appointment with a well-known specialist from Princess Margaret cancer hospital. He examined her and booked her for another surgery. After that surgery and Father Perna's prayers, Doris' cancer went into remission for ten years.

While living with Robert's family, Kaz again contacted Bishop Doyle. "He was kind and when he learned about our location, he put me in touch with a priest in the church of Bobcageon, Fenelon Falls, and Kinmount," Kaz recalled.

"We're going to find a use for you," the Bishop assured him. Soon afterwards, Kaz received a call from a priest in Fenelon Falls, who came to see them. "I want you two to move to Fenelon Falls," he said.

"We haven't got a place," Kaz pointed out.

"Don't worry. We have a place waiting for you," the priest assured them.

"What am I going to do when not able to walk properly?" asked Kaz.

"You'll use the telephone. That is what the Bishop told me." The priest was in charge of three communities. He visited the parishioners once a week. Kaz or Doris was to speak with them by phone and to begin visits to the nursing homes in the area.

One day, the priest gave Kaz a sign that read: 'Parish Rectory'. "This is for the outside door of your home office," he said. "You are now representatives of the church." The following Sunday morning, a lady knocked on that door and wanted to know what time the masses were held in the church. Kaz wondered what she thought about the pastor having breakfast in his house-coat.

Overall, Kaz and Doris enjoyed the work in the area even if moving was slow for Kaz because of his crutches. Every Sunday after the mass they went to a restaurant and ate German sausages which both of them liked.

Kaz said, "Father Perna knew my condition. 'Kaz, believe it,' he told me 'The Lord is going to heal you!' I was listening but was still like St. Thomas, asking, 'Show me the wound to put my finger in!' The good Lord listened to his petition, not my doubts. When working in Fenelon Falls I felt that something good was happening in my body. Soon, I was able to leave the crutches and rely on canes.

"I read a book about the power of God. When you pray for something, asking God to help you, be very specific. In my case, I used to have swollen 'plums' on the knuckles of my fingers and knew they were signs of rheumatoid arthritis, in which the tendons and muscles become inflamed. Father Perna was praying for my rheumatoid arthritis.

"Eventually, I am not sure what year it was, we moved to work in Lindsay and settled in an apartment on Angel Line. Father Moran handed me the keys to every parish building. He helped us in many ways and invited us to visit the rectory every Sunday. Eventually, we became acquainted with the nursing homes and found volunteers to help us. We were doing very well and I was functioning in the full capacity as a deacon."

The Golden Years

Kazimierz and Doris Chomko

May 7th, 2000

Kazimierz and Doris Chomko

Married June 10th, 1950

Robert and Lisa came to Kaz's and Doris' place for brunch every Sunday. One day, much to everyone's surprise, Richard showed up and said, "I have found a nice retirement home for you!"

"Oh, retirement! There is no such a word in our vocabulary, is there Kaz?" asked Doris.

"No, of course not," agreed Kaz. "But where and what is it, Richard?" Kaz inquired, out of curiosity.

"It is in Thornhill. The place is called Hesperus Fellowship Community and it was built a few years ago. At first, in order to live in this community, you had to buy a life lease. However, many who wanted to move there did not have the required financial resources because they were former teachers of the nearby Waldorf School which did not offer pension plans. Elizabeth and I did not want to buy because we wanted to have the money to help you when needed. Since the plan for life leases did not work out, these same apartments are now available for rent."

The following week, Kaz and Doris drove to Thornhill to see this unusual retirement home and the apartment intended for them. They liked what they saw.

At that time, Hesperus was under modification and going through financial challenges. Its Board of Directors had approached the provincial government for help. A representative of the Minister of Community and Social Services came to examine the place. He told the board members that the ministry would help, provided Hesperus met the government standards.

When Kaz and Doris visited Hesperus in the spring of 1991, the manager said, "We are under construction to meet the government standards. I suggest you move in the fall."

Kaz remembered well the day they moved in. "The place was still in an awful mess. A bulldozer had to be used to clear a path in order to unload our things from the truck. On the following Sunday, we were ready to go to church. When Doris stepped out to go to the car, she sank to her ankles in mud. She had to wash her boots before we left."

Of course, moving is always a challenge. First of all, transferring the belongings is not always straight forward – as Kaz and Doris experienced. Settling in, organizing the living space, cooking, eating, arranging furniture, growing accustomed to unusual sounds coming through the windows or within the house can all be stressful.

To Kaz and Doris this was nothing new. They had moved so many times. They always managed to create a comfortable home. Both of them adjusted easily to the idiosyncrasies of people sharing the immediate environment and to the sounds which, for some people, would be unbearable, such as loud train whistles they had experienced in their first home.

'Retired' is not an appropriate word to describe the people living in Hesperus. Its community is based on the understanding that we have, at each stage of our lives, unique and valuable contributions to make to ourselves, to each other, and to the greater community.

While satisfying the practical requirements of living and working together, the residents want to retain their spiritual aims. Hesperus would not be the 'Guiding Evening Star' as its name implied, if the people living in it did not prove it in everyday life. Toward this end the staff and residents alike strive to make the community supportive of each member no matter his or her political, religious or social affiliations. Through this support, the weakened members are helped. Each one is encouraged on his or her individual spiritual journey.

Many inter-generational activities take place at Hesperus. For instance, kindergarten students from the Waldorf School come, carefully carrying eggs in their hands, to share with the residents. They have harvested them from their chicken coop in the community garden. Or, a class of fifth graders comes to practice reading with the individual elders who are very soon counted as their special friends. And, the children's choir, directed by Richard's wife, Elizabeth, performs for the parents and residents during the yearly festivals.

Members of Hesperus can work in a dedicated art room where their water colour paintings fill the walls. Kaz chose to learn wood carving and, from then on, produced small sculptures to give as gifts. Doris' specialty became embroidery. To this day, a beautiful hanging depicting St. Francis with his birds, adorns Kaz's residence.

But the most important aspect of their life in Thornhill was to carry out the deacon's duties of helping those in need. This work had always involved both of them. Kaz and Doris had worked, through the years, as a team and had accomplished much wherever they were stationed. From Hesperus, they visited the nearby hospital and nursing homes to give council and comfort. This continued until Kaz's mid-nineties when Doris' cancer returned and she passed on.

The power of faith has always worked for Kaz and although losing his life companion was a bitter experience, he continues to counsel those who cross his path with frankness, clarity, and compassion. He helps them reflect on what is fundamental in life: Where do we come from? Where are we going? How can we live the most purposeful life? Kaz is a joyful man who wants others to share in the joy of faith.

In his wedding homily for his granddaughter, Katrina, Kaz spoke about her perseverance. He recalled her, as the little girl, who had persistently knocked on her grandparent's door until it was opened, and how she had demonstrated the virtue of perseverance and careful choices throughout her young life.

Kaz told the young couple, "An additional secret for a successful marriage is not to take each other for granted, but to express gratitude and appreciation. I give you an example from my life with Doris. I used to get up first and when Doris came to the kitchen, I said, 'Good morning, dear. Welcome to this new day!'

"Doris used to answer, 'This is the day that the Lord has made. Let us rejoice and be glad in it!' We embraced with a kiss and that was the way we began our day."

Kaz's and Doris' marriage was in its fifty-sixth year when Doris passed.

Kaz's homily carried authority that touched the inner being. It reminded us that, as the children of one God, our job is to work inwardly in order to make that connection clear and bright. This means raising our minds and hearts toward the Almighty One at all times, while we work, play and rest. This form of prayer does not take much time and it can be done anywhere.

Addressing the young people as a married couple, Kaz encouraged them to live as an example to other young people. Many people do not realize that it takes three to be properly married: a man, a woman, and God. He reminded them that no problems are truly solved unless God is the central point. When this is remembered, all difficulties, joys and sorrows will be well tempered.

Kaz concluded his homily with the prayer of St. Francis of Assisi. I think it is also a fitting conclusion to the Kaz Chomko Story:

Lord, make me an instrument of your peace.
Where there is hatred, let me sow love;
Where there is injury, pardon;
Where there is doubt, faith;
Where there is despair, hope;
Where there is darkness, light;
And where there is sadness, joy,

O Divine Master,
Grant that I may not so much seek
To be consoled as to console;
To be understood as to understand;
To be loved as to love;
For it is in giving that we receive;
It is in pardoning that we are pardoned;
And it is in dying that we are born to eternal life.

Amen.

Made in the USA
Lexington, KY
21 April 2012